IN THE COMPANY OF WOLVES

Other books by Kevin Brophy

Autobiography
Walking the Line (Mainstream Publishing)

Fiction
Almost Heaven (Marino)

IN THE COMPANY OF
WOLVES

KEVIN BROPHY

MAINSTREAM
PUBLISHING

EDINBURGH AND LONDON

First published in Great Britain in 1999 by
MAINSTREAM PUBLISHING COMPANY (EDINBURGH) LTD
7 Albany Street
Edinburgh EH1 3UG

ISBN 1 84018 154 0

All photographs © *Wolverhampton Express & Star*

A catalogue record for this book is available from the British Library

Typeset in Cheltenham and Perpetua
Printed and bound in Finland by WSOY

DEDICATION

For my son, Adam

AUTHOR'S ACKNOWLEDGEMENT

A version of this work formed part of
my submission for my Master's degree course
at Bretton Hall, University of Leeds.

Contents

Introduction

If you are looking for objectivity, then this is not the book for you: shamelessly partisan, it is an extended love lyric-cum-ode to a team that has had a place in my heart since I was a boy in Ireland in the middle of the century.

Time and circumstances – and luck – eventually made it possible for me to write this book, an account of a journey I had long dreamed of undertaking: following the men in old-gold and black for an entire season.

Now that I have fulfilled my dream, I am both amused and astonished by my own temerity – and naivety – in attempting such a task. When I arrived in the Black Country in July 1998, I knew no one there. I had neither friends nor contacts. I had never been to Molineux and I could lay claim to no special knowledge of football. (I still can't, although, like every other fan, I can immediately finger whatever might be going wrong on the pitch and just as quickly prescribe a remedy. We could all do Colin Lee's job in our spare time . . .)

It says much for the kindness of a great many people that *In the Company of Wolves* was ever started, let alone finished.

I am especially grateful to Colin Lee. I was nervous about inviting myself to training sessions, but the Wolves gaffer never objected to my touchline presence at the Newbridge training ground. I was never asked to move along: my questions, however unwelcome they might have been on a fraught or frosty morning, were always listened to attentively and answered with courtesy.

The same goes for John Ward. With patience and good humour, John was always ready to explain the thinking behind some moves he had just put the players through.

I had no official standing whatever at Molineux yet both Colin and John never made me feel less than welcome. Believe me, when you're a stranger in town, that makes a helluva difference.

I found the same welcoming spirit throughout Molineux. John Richards made time to see me. Graham Hughes, club historian and one-man information service, willingly took me on the magic tour of the cups and the caps, the jerseys and the trophies. Dot Wooldridge, manager's secretary and mother of all the Wolves, helped me to find a flat that I could just about afford. When nobody else knew the answers you took your queries to Barbara at Reception . . .

Lorraine Hennessy, the club's Public Relations Officer, made me welcome in the press room. In these days of cheque-book journalism, public opinion has relegated journalists to the Snake-pit Conference (along with lawyers and estate agents) but among the Molineux press corps, I found only good company and good *craic*. Ian Willars of the *Birmingham Evening Mail*, doyen of that corps, is known to his colleagues as 'the Duke': for his gracious reception of this Irish intruder in their midst I can only say that he is truly deserving of his ducal sobriquet. News agency boss Ron Warrilow showed me the inside of the local Crown Court – possibly in a generous attempt to ensure my non-arrival there as an official 'guest' of the Crown; more importantly, Ron was equally generous with background information about his beloved Wolves. Ron's assistant, Tony Raybould, brightened many a moment in the press room with his tall tales and ready smiles – although you couldn't say the same for his racing tips.

David Instone, a Molineux reporter for Wolverhampton's own paper, the *Express and Star*, is perhaps the most influential scribe in the press box, but he too lent a helping hand; it was on David's welcoming coat-tails that I first set foot on the training ground at Newbridge. Ray Brown and Len Kruczek of Radio Wulfrun figure often in these pages: together we clocked up many companionable miles. However far you travelled, at the end of the journey you'd find Bill Hatton and Pete Moodie of *The Wolf*, setting up their radio gear with sellotape and good humour: John 'Fozzy' Hendley was always there too, tapping out his website news to Wolves fans around the world: their good-humoured company made all our journeys shorter.

Geoff Owen of Clubcall was another who made me welcome; it was always good to have the *craic* with Geoff, whether in the press room or over a pint in a well-chosen hostelry. Bill Howell of the *Sunday Mercury* and Ged Scott of the *Birmingham Post* were another pair of distinguished journalists who kindly shared with me their extensive knowledge of the Black Country's superior watering-holes.

Naming names is dangerous: you always leave someone out. I hope it will be enough to say that meeting the people in that Molineux press room from week to week made my task easier and my life more interesting.

So did all the other folk I met: the stewards; the newspaper vendors; the guy selling fanzines at the back of the Stan Cullis; the fellows who guarded the car-park; people on the coaches. And fans – fans in transit at motorway service centres up and down the land, fans from here to Huddersfield, from Swindon to Sunderland: without them the game could not be beautiful.

I think it was Ged Scott of the *Post* who was winding me up one evening about the lack of objectivity in my writing. I was, Ged told me, just 'a fan with a pen'. It's an accusation to which I gladly plead guilty.

1

Beginnings

David Kelly of Tranmere Rovers kicked off the 1998–99 league campaign at Molineux. Some 20,000 fans roared in the afternoon to mark the moment. There was hope and pride – and perhaps even a little anger – in those voices baying at the August sun. These fans had been there the year before and the year before . . . and all the years before. So much had been promised, so little delivered: a Cup run ended by an Arsenal goal in the semi-final the previous year; a league campaign that ran out of steam in the Division One play-offs the year before that.

Wolves are a big club, with what the tabloids call 'a glorious past'. It was that past – umbilically linked with my own past, my boyhood years on the west coast of Ireland – that had drawn me to Molineux: it was part of the endless faith and hope that continued to draw the thousands of supporters around me to this patch of green on Wolverhampton's Waterloo Road. And part of the anger. Frustration anyway. What *was* a club like Wolves doing in the Nationwide First Division? Wolves *belonged* in the Premiership. Everybody knew that, except perhaps West Brom supporters (but then, as I was to learn quickly in Wolverhampton, West Brom supporters don't know a lot about anything).

You could only hope that the players on the pitch knew it as well as the rest of us. Better, anyway, than the various combinations that had worn the famous old-gold shirts for the best-forgotten years of the '80s and '90s to date. It was exactly 40 years, for God's sake, since Wolves had claimed the old First Division Championship; it was 14 years since we had even played in that old top division.

I have slipped into 'we': the truth is that objectivity, for Wolves followers evaluating their own team, is a counterfeit currency: the coinage of all great loves is passion.

Love was certainly in the air that Saturday afternoon, the first of a new season, as Tranmere set out their hopeless stall. To be sure, there were empty swathes in the yellow tiers of the John Ireland stand opposite me, and I had heard the stories about season-ticket sales being substantially down on last season's, but Molineux was still packed enough and partisan enough to make the Tranmere players wish they had begun their season in kinder surroundings. Was it terror or tactics that had driven them into an American football-style huddle before the kick-off, as though they might draw strength from their locked arms and huddled heads?

It didn't work. From the start, Wolves tore into them: there were old demons to be exorcised. The crowd bayed – for goals, for yesterday, for today and for the tomorrow we had promised ourselves. The goal when it came, after 20 minutes, was scored, inevitably, by Robbie Keane. His shot, from a pass by the Australian, Kevin Muscat, was parried by Tranmere's £5-million man, the teenage goalkeeper, Simonsen, but Keane himself struck the rebound home.

'There's only one Keeno!' the exultant crowd chanted.

Keane, himself a teenager like the keeper he had beaten, took a few moments to celebrate his goal with his team-mates before getting on with his game. So young, so slight . . . and yet he moved with such nonchalant ease on this English stage as if he had been born to it: they might have been those boys in the vast housing estates where he had grown up, in Tallaght, south west of Dublin.

It wasn't all Wolves after that, but it might as well have been. After 27 minutes our defence was sliced apart but, with Stowell, our keeper, helpless and beaten, the shot from Russell came back off the crossbar. We knew then, for sure, that the old Celestial Director of Football was on our side.

I was mesmerised by it all, by this explosion of love and desire in this so-called 'golden palace'. I listened and I felt and I watched, absorbing the faces and shapes and skills of men whose names, over the coming season, would become as familiar to me as the names of my own children.

Stowell, blonde and rugged, in goal. In front of him, Richards ('Deeno' to the crowd), Emblen and the imperious Curle. Across the middle of the pitch: Muscat, Robinson, Osborn, Corica and Froggatt. And up front, the goal-hunters, Robbie Keane and Steve Bull.

Keane was young, on the threshold of a career that could be long and prosperous and probably far-flung. Bull was coming to the end of a long and successful footballing life, almost all of which had been spent with Wolves. He had scored more goals for Wolves than any other player in history; a few years ago, when he was in his prime and playing for England, he passed up on the chance to move to a Premiership side, preferring to stay on with Wolves. Molineux loved him for his loyalty, his goals, his refusal ever to go gently into that ungodly night of defeat or that half-night of draws.

Bully didn't score in that first game of the new season, but they chanted his name anyway and he put himself about on the pitch with the constructive energy of a youngster half his age. Keith Curle, our captain, scored the second goal. When Froggatt was brought down in the penalty area, moments from the end, Curle lashed the resulting penalty into the roof of the Tranmere goal. His reported pre-season demand for a transfer (despite rumoured earnings of £5,500 a week plus bonuses) was forgotten and forgiven by the adoring crowd. Now they reminded him with gusto: 'There's only one Keith Curle!'

Curle's goal was the last significant action of the match. The team left the pitch to appreciative applause from all sides of the ground. The excitement was palpable but so, too, was the sense of relief: at least we had not come down at the first fence of the long, gruelling marathon that makes up the First Division season. (Teams play 46 games in the league season, eight more than in the Premiership.)

Listening to my neighbours in the Billy Wright stand, I thought I detected a lip-biting determination not to get carried away by this good start: I overheard one supporter, grinning, ask his companion if this was 'another false dawn'. Behind his words I could sense the remembered promises and the dashed hopes.

At the after-match conference Mark McGhee was also low-key. Like any manager unwilling to offer hostages to fortune, he reminded the assembled journalists that it was a good start but no more than that: the road (to the unmentioned goal of promotion) was a long one.

John Aldridge, the Tranmere manager, was smiling and graceful, as I'd expected him to be. Like most of Ireland, I have a deep, soft spot for this Scouse–Irishman who wore the Irish shirt with success and distinction for almost two decades. Watching Aldo field questions with the same grace and style that had endeared him to us all, I almost wished that this honorary Irishman had something more than defeat to take back with him to Tranmere on the road north from Molineux.

But only almost. You cannot forget who you are and where you come from. I was Irish and green, yes, and would never choose to be anything else, but at the heart of Molineux, I was old-gold and black, and I was in the company of Wolves.

I was brought up in the army barracks on the edge of Galway, a tiny, then-sleepy city on Ireland's western coast. That military childhood I have described in an earlier book, *Walking the Line*, and retelling the tale here would be pointless. Yet it remains the starting-point for this tale of my journey with Wolves. (And, yes, I agree, it is the starting-point of all the other journeys of my life too, whether in the heart or in the world or in both.)

I was born a couple of years before the end of what we Irish call 'the emergency' but which the rest of the world insists on calling 'World War II'. I'm not sure who or what, apart from myself, was emergent at that time: my recollection of those days is, understandably, somewhat more than cloudy. My actual emergence into Ireland's (and the world's) emergency took place in my great-uncle's home, a terraced, bathroom-free house on Lucan Street in Castlebar, a small market town some 50 miles north of Galway. My mother's own home was at the far end of the terrace, which meant it had two distinct advantages: (a) it was semi-detached, and (b) it was the closest of all the houses on the street to the copper-headed water pump – none of the houses on the street was encumbered with indoor taps or running water. In later years, when I was dispatched from the barracks in the bacon factory van to spend my summer holidays at my grandmother's house in Lucan Street, this nearness to the pump was an advantage I greatly prized, as I drew bucket after white, enamelled bucket of water home for the washing of pots and dishes and clothes and, often, myself, in the scullery. (The ablutions of my grandmother and my two aunts, who both worked in the bacon factory, were conducted behind the closed door of their shared bedroom.)

Lucan Street was, in those mid-century days, a kind of Irish Coronation Street, a grey row of two-up-two-downs where everybody knew everybody and where everybody also knew their place in life. That place was pretty near the bottom of the heap. If you were lucky, like my Auntie Dot and Auntie Julie, you had a job in the bacon factory which allowed you to stand all day in wellingtons on the wet floors of damp, cold factory rooms. What my aunts did in the factory was, to my boy's mind, unknown and unknowable but, years later, watching Auntie Julie struggle in her hospital bed to hold and puff at a fag, I would see the sad and bitter harvest of those years in her grotesquely swollen and distorted hands and wrists and ankles.

Not that I would criticise the bacon factory even then, when she was propped in her bed at the Sacred Heart Home, gasping at the door of death. I was middle-aged, the father of children and the author of books, and I knew that my aunt both admired and loved me – but I knew too that a word of criticism would force her poor, twisted, arthritic body up onto the plumped pillows so that she might remind me, lovingly, of the facts of life and the virtues of loyalty and gratitude.

To have a steady job in Castlebar in that time was an occasion to give thanks to God. It saved you from the emigrant boat, from the labourer's and skivvy's life in London or Leeds, in Birmingham or Coventry . . . maybe even in Wolverhampton, although the name never featured in the Irish litany of the towns of exile. The weekly wages meant there was never a shortage of food on the table in the kitchen, pushed up against the small, shining window that looked out on the footpath and the pump; they meant too that it was no burden to go on paying the weekly rent to the agent of the street's never-seen landlord: Lord Lucan, who gave his name to the street where I emerged into life, was like God – invisible, omnipotent and omnipresent in the body of his vicar on earth, the rent-collecting agent. You paid your rent because it was what you were there for; the agent collected it because it was what he was there for. You knew your place in life and you were glad you had a place.

My mother's only brother, Uncle Tim, might have disturbed that undisturbable pattern of life had he chosen to. He was, by my mother's adoring and often-told account, bright and industrious at school. He won a scholarship to the local Brothers College and – probably at great cost to the economy of the Lucan Street household – he was allowed to take up that scholarship. He might have gone further, perhaps even moved elsewhere, after he finished his secondary schooling, but Uncle Tim chose not to. Instead, he too went to the bacon factory but it was to a desk job in the office that he went, not to the wet floor of the factory. Uncle Tim's was a 'good job' and he wore a collar and tie and a breast pocketful of fountain pens to prove it. When he married, he didn't move far, just to the other end of Lucan Street, a couple of doors from the blacksmith's forge. Maybe the world beyond that street was too frightening for Uncle Tim — or maybe he was just blessed with the contentment of knowing his own place in the world. He may even have stayed to please my grandmother: he was the apple of her flashing brown eyes. She would have hated to see him take the emigrant boat to England.

Granny Garvey's attitude to England was ambivalent. She pitied the unfortunate Irish souls who had to suffer there to stay alive but she adored the English monarchy. Once, flexing my puny nationalist muscles when I was nine or ten years old — and beginning to learn in school history classes of the many ills that England had showered upon us — I dared to scoff at the array of crowned heads in my grandmother's dresser. It was ridiculous, I announced, to display the kings and queens of England on the dinner plates and teacups of a truly Irish household.

Eamon de Valera, and the Brothers who schooled me, would have been proud of my protest. My grandmother, however, was never known to be short of a word. What did I know about England, she demanded in fury. Who kept her and her four small children alive when her husband was dead and nobody cared if the rest of them lived or died?

The way my grandmother saw it, it was the King of England himself who wrote her name and address and put the stamp on the envelope that brought her British Army widow's pension to Lucan Street. It was futile to point out to Granny Garvey that neither old King George nor his useless Queen sat at a desk and wrote out Mrs Michael Garvey, Lucan Street, Castlebar, Co. Mayo, on the brown envelope. I'd have been banished to the backyard with a clip on the ear for impertinence and my grandmother's ignorance would have gone on undiminished.

I held my tongue. It was one of my first lessons in the labyrinthine links that bind these two islands together.

My mother's father was a soldier in the British Army, a Connaught Ranger who served in the Great War. As a boy, I shared most of Ireland's uneasy feelings about these Irishmen who had fought for the English at the same time as Patrick Pearse was mounting his death wish, doomed rebellion against the English Crown in Dublin's GPO. There was something shameful about my grandfather's wearing of the enemy uniform, his acceptance of the King's shilling. Such information was best buried, never to be revealed to your pals at school or in the barracks in Galway.

Life taught me a little tolerance. I began to realise, grudgingly, that my grandfather had joined the British Army because he needed to earn a living: the army of that time would take you even if you were uneducated and unskilled. It took a little longer for me to find pride in being connected to this unknown soldier who was medically discharged in January 1918 to spend his few remaining years in a wheelchair in Lord Lucan's street. We never knew where he had served; all 'them foreign places' sounded the same to my grandmother. After my grandmother died, in the late 1960s, my grandfather's pay-book, which might have told us a thing or two about his wartime movements, finished up on a post-funeral cleaning-out pyre that was raised by my grief-stricken aunts.

We knew our soldier-grandfather through my mother's words and from the portrait that hung in the tiny sitting-room in Lucan Street. (It was a room that seemed to exist only for the purpose of being shined and polished: I never saw anybody sit down in there, not even on the lovely *chaise-longue* that also disappeared in some later cleaning-out bonfire). It was an enlarged black-and-white photograph, fading to sepia, that showed him seated with crossed legs on a straight-backed chair. He was a handsome man and I suspect he was a little vain too – you can tell from the unmilitary posture and the cigarette poised with studied nonchalance between his fingers. And you can tell it from his hat – in the portrait my grandfather has swapped his Connaught Ranger's headgear for an Australian bushranger's hat, the soft brim folded back to show off the fine forehead, the proud eyes, the cultivated moustache.

His poise and his self-awareness still enchant me: there's a copy of the portrait on the wall of my own home, alongside a full-colour copy of his medical discharge. On leave from some hellish front (there were no unhellish fronts in that carnage), at large in some foreign furlough town, my grandfather decided to take time out from the war to have his picture taken: I respect this man who decided that he should be immortalised in a photograph. Best of all, I love that Australian hat; there's a bolshie touch to it that speaks to my own soul. I'm a Tommy, yes, that hat shouts, but I'm still me, my own self, and I will not be strait-jacketed into anybody's uniform. You could tell me that maybe it was just the drink, a boozy exchange of headgear with some Aussie mate who, like my grandfather, was lonely and far from home – you could tell me that, but I wouldn't believe you. In my heart I know that there was a touch of the dandy about old-young Granda Garvey, a flash of flamboyance, a streak of irreverence that winks out at me from that fading portrait.

He died long before I surfaced into Ireland's emergency, yet I knew him well, this soldier-grandfather of mine. Why would I not? I am flesh of his flesh, DNA of his DNA. I know that if he had ever found himself in the divine presence of Lord Lucan – landlord – my grandfather would have known his place and doffed his cap and tugged at his forelock; but I know too that he would have known his own worth and his own beauty, no matter in whose presence he stood.

My grandfather would have understood why I set out on my Wolverhampton journey. He would have known that hills are there to be climbed and gates are there to be opened. He would have known that you must make your journey, to Wolverhampton or Wipers, to Grimsby or Gallipoli, because the road in front of you is there to be travelled.

I like to think, too, that he would have understood that one journey's end is no more than another journey's beginning; a halting-place, a breather on the way. He would have known that all journeys begin and end in yourself.

Because that unknown soldier is part of who I am, I choose to begin with him my journey with Wolves. In him are joined the past and the present; in him and in me the past and the present of Ireland herself are joined: an English soldier and an Irish writer.

He's long gone, my grandfather; so too are his wife and all his children – my mother, my aunts, Uncle Tim and his fountain pens. The old house in Lucan Street, like Lord Lucan himself, has disappeared from the face of the earth. But not from my heart. It's alive, here, in these words, on this page.

So too is Granda Garvey, supping a pint after a game at Molineux, sitting beside me on the supporters' coach as we journey on the motorways of England to away games with the Wolves.

2

A Place in the Scheme of Things

'Who's Kevin Brophy?'

The fellow posing this millennial question was stooping in the press section, reading my name from the white paper sticker that the Barnet press people had taped to the upturned plastic seat.

I stood a moment in the gangway of the crowded area, taking in the questioner and his loud assertive voice. The tone of the voice was querulous too: it was obvious that the fellow would like to beam me up or out somewhere – anywhere – so that the dark-haired, good-looking woman standing beside him might take the seat next to his.

The packed stand had no answer to this fellow's question: at ten minutes to kick-off in what was a plum cup-tie for the club, the Barnet stands and their occupants had other questions on their minds. I watched the girl spread her hands in a gesture of acceptance. She backed away from the fellow, smiling at the journalists who stood up to let her pass.

It was a fabulous smile, the kind that would soften any wandering Irishman's heart.

'It's my seat in there,' I said, when she had edged out on to the gangway beside me, 'but I'll be glad to swap with you.'

The smile deepened. She shook her head. 'Thanks, but there's no need.' The dark, lustrous hair tossed around her shoulders as she moved to an aisle seat a few rows further down.

Her would-be companion's face did not soften as I announced that I was, indeed, the owner of the name on the sticky piece of paper and took my seat beside him.

His own name he chose not to reveal – or maybe he thought I should recognise him. He was young and good-looking; his legs were on tanned display in khaki shorts. He was a radio producer, he told me, although he didn't bother to say with which station; maybe that too was something I'd be expected to know. White Hart Lane and Highbury were his usual beat; his talk was littered with the names of famous Spurs and Gunners. While he talked, I noticed that his glance strayed often towards the dark-haired girl below us.

You'd be forgiven for thinking that our green-and-white-shirted Wolves were also distracted by this woman's raven-haired beauty. Certainly they had something on their minds, other than this first-round, first-leg tie of the League Cup. It was a game that Wolves might have expected to win with ease but they looked distinctly uncomfortable on the sloping pitch at Underhill. It wasn't that they couldn't create chances; they simply weren't able to put them away. Robbie Keane might have had three goals in the first half; Osborn's powerful shot, just on half-time, beat Harrison in the Barnet goal but came back off the crossbar. You could almost sense the kind of night it was going to be.

And it was. Halfway through the second half, Mike Stowell fumbled a harmless cross and McGleish headed Barnet in front. Although Osborn levelled with the best strike of the match – a lovely shot curled high and true into the far corner of the net – Currie was in at the death to make it 2–1 for Barnet.

David Instone of Wolverhampton's daily, the *Express and Star*, caught my eye after the final whistle. 'You'll get used to it, following Wolves,' he said, and I remembered the 'false dawn' comment after the Tranmere game.

David had given another journalist and myself a ride down from Wolverhampton for the game: it seemed a long way to come to be beaten. Yet, in one way, I was glad: better to learn early the taste of long-distance defeat.

Despite the defeat, the journey north on the M1 was companionable. I sat in the back, listening to David and Ged test each other with football-trivia questions as the dark miles fell behind us. I was astonished by their grasp of the game's minutiae, of players past and present, from the highest to the lowest reaches of the game. For a moment I almost envied them their knowledge but then I remembered that I had served no apprenticeship, as they had, on the back pages of provincial newspapers the length and breadth of Britain. It was enough to be there, sharing that easy, masculine warmth in the small car, trying to figure out the names of all the league clubs that had an 'X' in them . . . I wondered if my radio producer neighbour at Barnet had found any dark-haired comfort after the game. Or any kind.

★

The second leg of this cup-tie, a week later at Molineux, was a rout. Robbie Keane scored two, the second an impertinent, lazy scooping of the ball over mesmerised Barnet heads into the net, but the night belonged to Bully. He scored three; the ecstatic crowd would have crowned him emperor of somewhere, anywhere, on this magic night. Barnet were out-thought and out-fought but we applauded them generously as they left our personal field of dreams, beaten 6–2 on aggregate. They had been reminded of their natural place in the scheme of things and, in the warm Wolverhampton night, we were prepared to pardon them their upstart notions of the previous week.

3

Black Country Bliss

In between these two League Cup legs, we had an away league game at Oxford. I travelled down on the Friday, gently but fervently encouraging my elderly Kadett along the slow lane of the M5, then east along the M42 before taking the M40 south. I was far down the M40 when I eased the old thing out into the middle lane to overtake a long line of barely moving vehicles ahead of me; too late I realised that I was overshooting Junction 9, that the almost-stationary cars and trucks were waiting to get off the motorway and on to the A34 for Oxford. No matter: the enforced map-reading stop at the next junction gave me the chance to visit the new services megalopolis behind the A40. It was also a reminder of what to expect at commuter-hour on Britain's motorways.

I spent the weekend with my sister and her husband in Abingdon, just south of Oxford. I sat with my brother-in-law and hundreds of other

Oxford season-ticket holders in the Beech Road stand of the Old Manor ground. In the Saturday afternoon sunshine you could almost touch the optimism of the home supporters. It was easy to understand that optimism: Wolves had never won at the Manor – in their nine visits to the ground they had managed only four draws and five defeats. Although they had been held to an away draw in their opening game against newly promoted Bristol City, Oxford fans had been cheered by a first league goal from their record £400,000-signing from Aberdeen, Dean Windass, and I was assured by my brother-in-law that I'd be going home empty-handed.

The game was ill-tempered, littered with niggling fouls and questionable refereeing decisions. The Oxford players, in their canary-yellow shirts and black shorts, were infuriated by the ref.'s decision to allow our first goal. Almost on half-time, Bull went up with Whitehead, the Oxford keeper, for a high Muscat cross; Whitehead was hustled to the ground and, as the ball squirted loose, Bully booted it home. Salt was rubbed into the angry Oxford wound seconds later when, at the other end, Stowell failed to gather the ball but was awarded a free kick against the attacking Murphy for an illegal charge. I kept my mouth shut at half-time in the Beech Road stand.

In the second half the yellow cards went on flashing as tempers became more ragged in the heat. Half an hour into the half the yellow changed to red for Davis's foul tackle on Robbie in the penalty box. The canary-shirts squawked in protest, Curle kicked and Whitehead saved but, before the home fans could applaud his exploit, Osborn had poked the ball into the Oxford net. A flukey goal, the brother-in-law muttered, but I generously refrained from shaking my triumphant fists in his face: there's no such thing as a bad goal for your own side. Anyway, I knew that it was my Irish presence that had inspired Wolves to this first-ever win at the Manor.

We lingered a while in the ground after the final whistle; I was in no hurry to leave the scene of a tasty 2–0 win (it's remarkable the ease with which bad tempers – and bad decisions – can be cast in a kinder light by such a result). On the way out, the brother-in-law pointed out, just ahead of us, one of Oxford's most eminent supporters – the author Desmond Morris, and his kaftan-clad other half. Never missed a home game, the brother-in-law said with a touch of proprietary pride. Old Desmond was probably conducting a long-term study of naked losers, I figured, but that thought, too, I generously kept to myself. Wolves were on a roll: two games, two wins and not a goal conceded.

★

Football is rarely short of irony. When the programme for the home game against Swindon was being printed, it probably seemed a good idea to put Neil Emblen on the cover; by the time match day arrived, however, Neil had been relegated to the subs' bench and his place given to Steve Sedgley. In a way, I was sorry for the change: Neil's periodic charges up the middle of the field, from deep in his own half well into opposition territory, were a fair-haired sight to behold. Maybe such a cavalier approach was the reason he found himself on the bench; then again, maybe Sedgley was the better footballer.

There were other changes, too. Fernando Gomez, a former Spanish international, had joined Wolves from Valencia and, after making his first appearance against Oxford, looked like becoming a fixture as our midfield playmaker. Fernando covers the ground with an easy lope that looks almost lazy, even indifferent; he's the same on the ball – he dawdles on it, looking around before dispatching it. Molineux relished his intelligence, the sureness of his touch – time and again we put our hands together to applaud our new Spanish midfielder. David Connolly had also joined, from Dutch side Feyenoord. Although Connolly had been capped 13 times for Ireland, he was going to have to fight for a starting place up front: Robbie Keane was winning the attention of the national press and Bull didn't look like a man who would happily hand over his striker's shirt. Connolly started the Swindon game on the bench, alongside Emblen and Corica.

The game was decided by a single penalty. Half an hour into the first half Robbie Keane, rampaging into the Swindon penalty area, was brought down by Ty Gooden, and Curle slotted the resulting penalty home.

Afterwards, in the Molineux press room, I listened to Steve McMahon, the Swindon manager, rail against the bad fortune that had given his side nothing from a game which they had dominated for most of the time. Obviously Steve and I had not been watching the same match. Like the journalists crowding the small room, I kept my disagreement to myself: McMahon, balding and glowering, did not look like the kind of fellow you ought to disagree with.

Anyway, it was three wins out of three championship games – and still not a goal conceded.

★

The following Friday night, away to Watford, we made it four out of four. It was the start of the August Bank Holiday weekend, so the fleet of coaches pulled out of Molineux car-park early that afternoon. It was my first experience of travelling by supporters' coach.

I loved it. What I felt must be the way nudists feel, who stumble, unfigleaved, on to a naturist beach which is covered with similarly leafless bodies. My fellow travellers on the coach were clothed to be sure, in varying garb of gold and black but their colours served only to make their madness – their passion – all the more naked. I had been among them at Molineux but to share this journey was an altogether deeper experience. This was a pilgrimage, but with a difference: the shrine we travelled towards was the personal madness each one of us took with us, a madness which altered and was altered by the very acts of sharing and travelling. We were missionaries but we did not travel to proselytise: at the end of every such away journey awaited some lunatic bunch of home fans who were, incredibly, convinced of the superiority of *their* brand of insanity. Rather, we were conquistadors, with conquest – and league points – on our Molineux minds.

Put it another way: on that coach I was in hog heaven. I didn't have to listen to any London agent asking: 'For God's sake, why d'you want to write a football book?' Nor did I have to swallow my righteous anger towards some football know-alls back in Galway demanding: 'Wolves? A book about Wolves! Why don't you do [*sic*] a book about Arsenal [sicker] or United [sickest]?'

Instead, on this golden coach, here was Richard, large, crumpled and as insane as myself, enraptured after our exchange of identities. To him a book about Wolves was the only kind of book worth doing (no, it's not *sic* when it's spoken by one of your own). We had only just met, we were separated in age by more than 20 years, and we came from different countries – but we felt as though we had known each other all our lives.

The Watford PR lady had agreed to give me a press ticket so I left the fans at the coach park to make my separate way uphill past the allotments, to the main entrance. Night was falling; the Vicarage Road floodlights were on. Under their white glare, to the amusement of the large crowd, the home side's mascots, Harry and Harriet, were married before the kick-off to the loud-speakered strains of Mendelssohn's *Wedding March*. Our own mascot, Wolfie, was on hand. High up in the glass lean-to that is Watford's press box, I wondered what the composer would make of this use of his music. Most likely the august presence of the black and gold would soothe him. Elgar, after all, had been a Wolves fan: one class act sitting in the stand recognising his equals on the pitch.

Obviously, that other composer, the Watford chairman, didn't rate the scribes and journalists of the modern media as 'class'. Having seen and heard Sir Elton bitching in a TV documentary about standards in a 95-star hotel in France, it was impossible to imagine him enduring the cramped, stifling quarters of the Vicarage Road glasshouse. Yes, I know I'd been given a free press ticket but that doesn't mean I left my few discerning brain cells behind in Wolverhampton. Insanity, after all, has its limits.

Class told on the pitch. Just on half-time, Keith Curle centred the ball to Froggatt, who pushed it out to Bull and he, in turn, drove it hard into the Watford net. Seconds later the half-time whistle blew. The interval cup of plastic tea tasted like good wine.

So good, in fact, that I lingered too long over it.

I was climbing the steps to the glasshouse, my back to the second-half kick-off, when my journalist neighbour shouted: 'Quick, Kevin! Look! Look!'

I turned but, like the Watford defence, I was not quick enough: the ball was already in the net, Robbie Keane was wheeling away in goal-scoring triumph and we were 2–0 up.

'There's only one Keeno!' the crowd chanted.

In the non-partisan sobriety of the press conservatory, I could only envy my fellow fans their untrammelled delirium.

It stayed 2–0 to the end, despite a couple of heart-stopping moments when Mike Stowell's hands went flapping in the floodlights in our goalmouth: the hands flapped and ended up maddeningly empty. Luckily so too did the Watford goal-bag.

I had a longer hike back to the coach area than the fans behind the Wolves goal, so I left the press section as soon as the final whistle was blown. The crowd was thinning out as I made my way downhill in the darkness, past the allotments. I couldn't tell, looking in over the metal fencing, what the tall green plants were . . . and yet I knew there were turnips thriving in those allotments. That tabloid title had been banished from our memory while Graham Taylor was, briefly, manager at Molineux but he no longer enjoyed such protection: nowadays Taylor was merely the manager of Watford. (By the end of the season, however, his dogged persistence with a mediocre side would win admiration up and down the land, wherever football is played.)

Nearing the coach, I fell into step with another laggardly Wolves supporter, labouring under the weight of a huge, black refuse sack slung over his shoulder. He turned out to be none other than the *alter ego* of Wolfie: the Disneylike outfit was in the black sack. And where, I wanted to know, was Wendy? Did she not get taken to away games? She was at home, he said with a tired smile, minding the house. We wished each other a safe journey home to the Black Country.

In the months to come I would have ample opportunity to taste the bitter fruits of defeated, pointless journeys back to Wolverhampton. On that August Bank Holiday Friday night, however, the coach was suffused with the warmth of victory, the contentment of three further points under our championship belt. The traffic jam on the M25 didn't matter; indeed, it served only to prolong our contented journey. When we eventually pulled into Waterloo Road, the stadium and car-park were bathed in a golden glow from the street lights. (On other nights they might be merely amber.) As we were getting off the coach, happily tired in the balmy night, I heard Richard, behind me, telling anyone who cared to listen, that he was afraid he was going to wake up in the morning and find that this glorious, unbeaten start was all just a dream.

I know how Richard felt. Throughout that long, hot August weekend I had to keep reminding myself that it was early days: four wins, even without conceding a goal, do not constitute promotion. And yet this was why I had come to Wolverhampton: to live out a boy's dream of hunting with the Wolves on the only trail that mattered – the road that led to glory.

I sensed the same dreaming hunger among the crowd at Molineux on the Monday, three days after our Watford win. Our visitors were Stockport County, but we all knew they were there only to make up the numbers. Mike Stowell was given a standing ovation for his four clean sheets as he took up his place in our goal. It took only six minutes for Dean Richards to put us in front, powering the ball home, low and true, from a corner.

The golden palace rocked and rolled to the singing of 'We're Gonna Win the League!' It rock 'n' rolled more when the giant TV screens flashed up the news that Grimsby were leading West Brom 3–0.

The stadium exploded into a carnival-like frenzy when Fernando, without so much as clicking a castanet, chested down a high ball and volleyed a long, dipping, unstoppable shot into the right-hand corner of the Stockport net. It was a stunning goal, the best I had yet seen.

Only 37 minutes gone, and we were 2–0 in front. Even the atheists among us knew that God was in his heaven and all was right with the world.

And then, incredibly, it started to go wrong. We were shifting in our seats, anticipating our half-time cuppa, when Angell rose with satanic intent to stain Stowell's unblemished sheet: his glancing header found the net and we had given away our first league goal. Eight minutes after the interval Angell again spread his demonic wings to boot the ball into our net. We had given away a two-goal lead and the pill was truly hard to swallow.

It ended like that. We put a brave face on it, spilling out on to the Waterloo Road, milling around Billy Wright's statue and the Stockport team bus. Stockport weren't a bad side we reminded ourselves, and one another and, anyway, only Sunderland's better goal-scoring record kept them ahead of us at the very top of the Division One table.

All winning runs, I told myself, making my way uphill to the car-park, must come to an end some time. And ours was still an unbeaten run. It was as much as – if not more than – I had dared to hope for at the beginning of the season: we were sharing top points with Sunderland, the promotion favourites, at the end of the first month. It wasn't a bad way to be finishing August.

Little did I – or any of my fellow fans heading home in the August evening – realise what September held in store for us.

4

The Road to Wolverhampton

It had been raining waterfalls the day in July that I left Galway, the Wednesday before Race Week. I could be fanciful and say that the heavens opened in sorrowing protest against my leaving this old home town of mine. The reality is more prosaic: it just rains a lot – an awful lot – in the west of Ireland. Yet the day had an apocalyptic feel about it: this rain pounded so fiercely against my old car and spilled in such huge torrents down the windscreen that, even at high speed, the wipers could barely keep the glass clear. I sat erect, intent on the grey, flooded road east, towards Dublin and the Irish Sea.

I'd taken time out from packing to say my farewells. The last goodbye had been that morning, to an old teacher of mine who had become a friend and a fan. Donal is a much-loved institution in Galway: teacher, storyteller and local historian. Long retired from a lifetime spent in the classroom, he still lectures at the local university to visiting bunches of Americans intent on discovering Irish 'culture' and, sometimes, their own Celtic roots. Donal's enthusiastic promptings to these groups keep my books ticking over in the town's bookshops. My last call on that torrential morning was to autograph a few books for American buyers in Donal's terraced house in the heart of the town.

While I signed the books and chatted to Donal, I was conscious of the deeper significance of this particular goodbye on this day of leaving. Donal was an important figure in my personal landscape; he had been an influential member of the school which, along with my home, had dominated my adolescence and shaped, for good and bad, the man I would become. The school's past pupils – 'old boys', as they might say in Wolverhampton – dominated the trades and the professions in the town; they also guarded the school's reputation with a fierce pride. That reputation was based on unquestioning discipline and unequalled exam results. The school took pride in producing doctors and engineers and scientists, with the occasional teacher, accountant or priest thrown in for variety, but had no truck with fancy-dan operators like writers, artists and actors. Somehow, amid such cheerful philistinism, Donal and one or two others like him managed to instil into young hearts a sense of something beyond money, beyond position, beyond property. His enthusiasm for rose windows raised youthful giggles; his love of old churches raised teenage eyebrows. Yet something of his innate love of the old and the beautiful took root in even the roughest of the boys who passed through Donal's classes over the decades: I have yet to meet an old Bishman who does not recall him with affection – sometimes grudging, but never denied.

I confess I am prejudiced. As far as that old school is concerned, I wear my heart on my sleeve and have always done so. The years I spent there were a time of discovery – of books and poems and words and ideas; of fresh dark hair on my groin and in my armpits; of girls and their soft skin and a first real kiss in the half light of the Dyke Road, up beside the darkening river.

If Donal had any misgivings about football and Wolverhampton as fit subjects for a writer's pen, he kept them to himself. We wished each other well before I dashed into the rain from his small, neat house in Woodquay. No forensic archaeologist would ever discover them, but that small street by the waterside and all the other narrow, curving streets of the town are stamped with the footprints and fingerprints of my life.

It was not the first time I had left the town. Going through school and university I had always taken it for granted that I would leave it. The wide world was waiting for me; I knew that it would welcome me. Instinctively I had known, too, that it was to England I would take myself. Unlike many of my contemporaries, I disdained the notion of heading west to America: it was too loud, too vulgar – and anyway neither Brophys nor Garveys had settled there so there was no family pull from that direction. I have no idea of where – or if – Grandfather Garvey travelled in England, although he almost certainly spent some time in the Connaught Rangers depot in Aldershot; nevertheless, it connects me somehow to that never-seen grandparent to think that sometime, somewhere, on my later travels in the UK I must have followed in his footsteps. The archaeology of the human heart is written – and deciphered – in feelings and memories and yearnings.

31

My first departures were no more than the beginnings of long, college summer breaks: in a warehouse in Leeds; on a building site outside Edinburgh; in Dickens & Jones department store beside London's Oxford Circus; to a resort hotel in Cornwall where I pot-walloped without enthusiasm but swam almost daily in the cold sea with a sense of wonder. I never made much money on these excursions; what I harvested, instead, was a sense of my own otherness, my own Irishness, and alongside that a realisation that Granny Garvey, although she had never set foot in England, had not been wrong: these people were like us but they were also decidedly different from us.

When I married, in 1967, it was to England that my Irish wife and myself headed. I taught English in the Potteries; I travelled 'on supply' among a number of schools in swinging London; and finally I fetched up at a now disappeared grammar school in Gidea Park in Essex. We moved back, first to Galway, then to Dublin, where I began to work in publishing. Children came, a son and two daughters; so too, through good fortune and hard graft, did money, cars, houses.

When the marriage ended after 20 years, I took flight again for London. I could not have named what I was searching for; very likely I didn't even know that I was searching for anything. I stayed for a couple of years, idling my way through the cinemas of the West End and the tree-lined thoroughfares of Maida Vale and Little Venice. Perhaps the films grew too dull; maybe my feet just got tired of all that aimless wandering. Whatever: I woke up one morning in my walk-up flat in Sutherland Avenue and I realised that I was going back to Galway.

That was in 1990. Now, eight years later, I was leaving again, guiding my old car on the rain-drenched roads towards Wolverhampton.

Nothing seemed to have changed – yet, in truth, a great deal had changed. In my years back in Galway, in the streets that had shaped me, I had gone back to my first and truest love: writing. I'd had no Archer-like success – I didn't expect it, for my kind of writing – but I'd enjoyed the tactile and intellectual pleasure of holding two of my own published books in my own hands. I had tasted, lingeringly, my good reviews; I had savoured, as discreetly as possible, the sight of my own books in bookshop windows.

The years between coming and going had made me a writer. This journey in the rain was about writing – it was the beginning of my commission to produce *In the Company of Wolves*.

Or maybe the beginning of that book — *this* book — went much further back. To the sodden streets I was leaving. To this frail, lovable old teacher who wished me Godspeed. To my own unseen fingerprints that not even this deluge could wash away.

That evening I sat with my son and my daughters in a plastic-and-chrome '50s-style diner in Blackrock, south Dublin, and let myself give in to the flow of their exuberant mickey-taking about my pathetic First Division team who couldn't win promotion to the Premiership. (The mickey-taking was unbarbed: on a trip to Dublin some weeks later my daughters were equally exuberant about my gifts of Wolves scarves.)

I stayed that night with a couple who were college contemporaries from the distant past in Galway. Everywhere I looked, it seemed, I was confronted by figures from my past. The thought stayed with me, driving me up the ramp of the ferry-cat at Dun Laoghaire next morning; I was journeying to another country, to a new beginning, but, as always, I was bound for the heart of my own past.

5

Brazen Larceny

That September, Wolves seemed determined never to recapture those early triumphs. As I watched one lifeless display after another throughout that long month, I couldn't help thinking that our heroes seemed almost frightened of taking both us and themselves back to the glory of our fabled past. Every last man (and woman and child too) of the Molineux faithful knew that Wolves had been born and bred to strut their stuff on the great football stages of England and beyond but, as we swallowed one disappointing result after another, we began to wonder if the current team had lost the plot. Maybe the breeze affects only the flight of the ball on the pitch; in the stands it is the pages of history that are stirred each Saturday afternoon.

Despite giving up a two-goal lead at home to Stockport on the last day of August, we entered September with an optimism that seemed well-founded. Only Sunderland ranked above us in the table, and that only because they had scored more goals than we had. Local rivals West Brom and Birmingham were a satisfying three points behind us; Bolton, Barnsley and Palace, the three teams relegated from the Premiership the previous season, languished even further below. Ipswich, who, like Sunderland, had featured and failed in the previous year's play-offs and had won only one of their opening five games, had six points to their credit, all of seven less than our total, and they stood a comforting 14 places below us in the table.

That dismal September would alter the shape of the table in a way that seemed only too familiar to the followers of the black and gold. We could rationalise our exit from the Worthington Cup; we could tell ourselves and one another that it was no bad thing to be finished with this knock-out competition, that now we could concentrate all our energies on the only goal that mattered – promotion to the Premiership. We could and we did comfort ourselves with such truths. The real truth still rankled: defeat had been dished out to us by lowly Bournemouth, so many places below us in the league pecking order that we couldn't be bothered to count them.

Back in Ireland for a few days and tidying up business, I had missed the first leg of this tie, a 1–1 draw in Bournemouth, but I was in my usual place in the Billy Wright stand on a chilly night in late September to see Bournemouth stem wave after wave of Wolves' attacks before returning to their southern coast with a well-deserved 2–1 victory in the bag, winning the tie 3–2 on aggregate. Bournemouth owed their win to a brilliant display by their keeper, Ovendale, and to confusion in the Wolves defence which bordered on the schoolboyish. The tiny troop of Bournemouth fans were ecstatic, the Molineux legions less so – Wolves were booed off the pitch at half-time and again after the final whistle. You could say it was unkind, but Wolverhampton football folk have their own concepts of chivalry and courtesy: the stands stood to applaud the red-and-black striped footballers of Bournemouth off the Molineux turf.

By then, too, we had slipped from our lofty league perch alongside Sunderland. In that long September, beginning away to Port Vale on the 8th and ending at home to QPR on the 30th, we played a total of five league games. We won only one of these games; we drew another one;

most distressingly, we lost three. Out of a possible 15 league points, we harvested a mere four. A record which, at the end of August, had read 13 out of 15 points, was changed by the end of September to 17 out of 30.

★

The rot started at Port Vale.

In fact, judging by the appearance of the streets as our supporters' coach nudged its police-escorted way through the evening traffic, the rot had been going on for a long time in the Potteries. Through the windows of the coach we stared at a bleak, post-Thatcherite vista of boarded-up, cemented windows and doorways in abandoned houses whose roofless tops gaped at the evening sky like open mouths aghast with decaying teeth. 'For Sale' or 'To Let' boards seemed to sprout like hopeless molars from every deserted home and shut-down shop. What could you sell here, I wondered, and who would buy from you in this barren, post-holocaust landscape?

The only selling Wolves did that night was to sell themselves short. Port Vale were the bottom club in the division; from five games they had managed only a single draw. They should have been passable fodder for our Wolves but it was Vale who did the better scavenging in the unfinished ground. After 14 minutes Stowell was beaten, rather ridiculously, by a 30-yard shot from Beadle. Ten minutes into the second half, with Wolves pressing almost incessantly, Vale broke upfield to score another fortuitous goal.

I watched, disbelieving, from the garden-hut press box, as we failed to put away chance after chance. Robbie got one back for us halfway through the second half but, try as Wolves might, you always felt that Vale would hold out. The gods of sport write their own commandments: sometimes David *does* take the head off Goliath. Maybe the same gods had been offended by Fernando's bright red cycling shorts: two minutes after the kick-off he'd been sent to the sidelines by the referee because their knee-length redness clashed, illegally, with the dark Wolves' shorts.

When I left the hut after the final whistle, the night was cold and bitter. I picked my way carefully across the rubble-strewn flat roof, towards the yellow metal staircase that led to the ground. Maybe, after all, we had merely lost our footing on this chilly September night? One false step, my coach companion and myself agreed, didn't necessarily mean we were on a downhill slope.

★

But we were.

Five days after the defeat at lowly Port Vale, we took on Sunderland at Molineux. The northerners were everybody's promotion favourites in the division: the previous May, in a heartbreaking play-off final at Wembley, they had drawn 4–4 with Charlton after extra time before losing 7–6 on penalties. Their manager, Peter Reid, reputedly a 'hard man', had not only kept faith with his beaten players but had managed to inspire in them a determination to do even better next time, no small accomplishment after such a dose of gall. The Wolves fans recognised the significance of the game: almost 27,000 of us were packed into our golden palace. We were at full strength on the pitch too, which was reassuring, although personally I was disappointed that Irish international Niall Quinn was not fit enough to line out with Sunderland.

We could have been comfortably ahead by half-time. Bull missed a sitter, shooting over the bar from close range after two minutes. Ten minutes later he headed over again from a long Muscat centre. Robbie, too, appeared to have lost his touch: on the half-hour he found himself through with only the keeper to beat but his tame shot was easily saved by Thomas Sorenson. And there was more bad luck: in the 35th minute a screaming 40-yard shot from Naylor had everyone beaten but came back off the bar. Despite our dominance, it was still scoreless at the interval.

Robbie finally unjangled our nerves halfway through the second half when he capitalised on a mistake by defender Michael Gray – the unfortunate player who had missed his penalty in the Wembley shoot-out – to slot the ball home from close range. Once more the heavens were lifted with chants of 'Keeno! Keeno!' It was bliss, in that moment, to be alive but to be a Wolves man was very heaven . . . the favourites beaten, three points in the bag . . . what more could you ask for?

For starters, a referee who didn't play an eternity of unnecessary time added on.

We were, by my watch, in the 49th minute of the second half when, after a bout of head-tennis in a confused Wolves goalmouth, Kevin

Phillips nodded home the equaliser from close range. The lower deck of the John Ireland stand was loud with northern hosannahs; a sea of red-and-white banners swelled and roared in our Molineux afternoon.

We were silent and silenced. This was brazen larceny. We were masters on the pitch, the points were ours: how had we allowed a pair of them to be snatched from our grasp in the dying seconds of the game? It was a draw that tasted like a defeat.

6
Captain Bird's-Eye of Huddersfield

Worse was to come the following Saturday in the warm sunshine at Huddersfield. It was a glorious afternoon, the kind of day on which unchained wolves should roam free over Yorkshire prairies – or, in our case, deal summarily at the McAlpine Stadium with a team of upstart terriers. Huddersfield Town were masquerading as league leaders: their presence at the top of the table, we all agreed, was a typical early season glitch, the kind of statistic you'd look back on at the end of the season with a wry smile and you'd shake your head and say, wonderingly, 'Well, imagine that! Town at the top!'

Wolves, we agreed, would restore some sanity to the table – not to mention restoring Huddersfield to a more appropriate position in it. We were in high spirits, driving up the M6 and turning east on the M62: today's encounter with these disrespectful table-toppers would put the Sunderland disappointment into a more acceptable perspective. I was travelling with Ray and Len, a couple of volunteers who did commentary for Radio Wulfrun's patients in New Cross Hospital back home in Wolverhampton. Over the months ahead Ray and Len would become my travelling companions for many of our away games: God only knows how many millions of words we spent together throughout the season on pre-match analysis and homeward-bound post-mortems. Some journeys – Carrow Road and the Stadium of Light come to mind – we made with not a little trepidation but, heading towards Huddersfield on that brilliant Saturday, our mood was upbeat.

For myself there was also a personal kind of connection with Huddersfield Town. In the 1980s, in another existence when I had been a publisher in Dublin, I had published the autobiography of Eoin Hand, Jack Charlton's predecessor as manager of the Irish international side. Eoin was what old Dubliners might call 'a darlin' man' – the kind of fellow who'd go out of his way to do you a good turn. He was also an effective but ultimately luckless international manager who never got the rub of the green: bad bounces, wretched refereeing decisions and bizarre results from elsewhere meant that, under Eoin, Ireland never qualified for the finals of a European or World championship. Eoin deserved better than the crucifixion he endured at the hands of a small section of the Dublin media. When his international career ended, Eoin first tried his hand at club management in Saudia Arabia before returning to England as manager of Huddersfield. I'd met him after a game at Craven Cottage in, I think, 1989: he was still buoyant, still enthusiastic as ever . . . and still dogged by the same ill luck. He took Huddersfield to the brink of promotion one season and they teetered there a while before slipping back into mid-table obscurity.

I had always liked Eoin; by illogical extension I was also prepared to like Huddersfield Town. And, truly, they were easy to like . . .

When Ray drew to a halt in the supporters' car-park, the neighbouring car was disgorging a couple of blue-and-white clad teenagers who took off in a hurry: you could smell the chips and burgers they had on their minds. The driver of the car set about his business in more leisurely fashion, checking the doors, removing his tote bag (of sandwiches and tea?) from the boot. He too was wearing the blue-and-white stripes of Town, but what struck me most about him was the bright eyes that twinkled above his grey beard: with his generous paunch he looked like some Captain Bird's-Eye who was taking his crew ashore for the day.

'It's a great day for it,' I said, standing beside him, retrieving my own bag from the back of our car.

'Aye.' The twinkling eyes swept the hills, came back to rest on my bag, on the metal cases of gear that Ray and Len were lining up on the tarmac. 'You're covering the match?'

'The lads are,' I said, nodding towards Ray and Len. 'I'm doing a book myself . . .'

He listened intently as I told him, briefly, of my lunatic assignment, the move from Galway, the miles covered and still-to-be travelled. I knew from the way his eyes went on twinkling and the grizzled head went on nodding that I was talking to a fellow lunatic. My tale took only a minute or two; when I had finished, he began to tell us about himself. He'd been born and bred in Huddersfield; he had been a Town supporter all his life. Work had taken him to Crewe but, for some 20 years, he'd been a regular supporter at all of Town's games. Some away games too, he said, but it wasn't always easy, given the cost of season tickets and travel: even in the bright Yorkshire sunshine you could never escape the price of your dreams. We walked together down the hill from the car-park and around the bend to the stadium entrance, and we went on talking as if we had known one another all our lives – and in a sense we had. He remembered my friend Eoin's tenure as manager with affection but it was for Peter Jackson that his special pride was reserved. 'He's taken us to where we are,' the captain said, 'and he'll take us further – just wait and see.' It would have been churlish to disagree with this gracious man, so we shook hands and wished each other luck and headed for our separate entrances.

The main entrance and reception area of the McAlpine Stadium are what you'd expect of such a ground – spacious and classy and very much aware of its own classiness. And the sense of ambition there is so palpable that you feel you can wrap it up and stow it in your shoulder bag, along with your notebook and Saturday's *Guardian*. Our own Molineux is just as elegant but here they seemed more impressed – perhaps astonished – at finding themselves in the middle of such elegance. I was glad that Ron had taken me aside the previous Saturday at Molineux to advise that there was a 'dress code' in the press box at Huddersfield, that my usual gear of jeans and open-necked shirt might not be quite the thing at the McAlpine . . . We passed men wearing navy blazers and corporate cufflinks and racehorse-sleek women wearing expensive smiles and expensive hair-dos as we crossed the directors' landing to reach the press area.

It was still early, maybe an hour to kick-off. Peter Jackson was down below us on the sideline, talking to a couple of corporate suits. A young local journalist pointed him out to me but I'd have recognised him anyway from his picture in the papers, this youngster from nowhere who'd taken the club from the very same place to the top of the table. Minutes later, at my own request, I was being introduced to Peter

Jackson. With his neatly trimmed hair, mischievous blue eyes and boyish good looks, he'd pass for the Head Prefect or the captain of the First Cricket XI of some 1950s grammar school. His manner, too, was prefect-like in its courtesy and enthusiasm: he shook my hand, bade me welcome, listened to my questions as if there might be a grain of sense in them. He had no trumpet to blow about his team's success; he was enjoying it and hoped it would continue. The stands were filling up slowly around us as he stood there on the terrace, a young man content and complete in himself, careless of his team waiting below stairs for the inevitable last-minute words. Maybe that was part of his motivational success – that, while he was with you, you deserved and got his undivided attention. And when you were gone, you were gone . . . Peter Jackson, and men like him, shake hundreds of hands like mine every week: their memory, of necessity, must be fitted with some automatic refuse disposal unit. Something else struck me, as Peter headed for the dressing-room with a last cheery smile and a wave: the vision and courage of the club's controllers, who could entrust the destiny of their multi-million-pound operation to such a laughing schoolboy. (Neither Peter nor I could tell on that sunny Saturday that, just a few months later, on the last day of the season, he would be unceremoniously booted out of his managerial chair at Huddersfield. Frailty, thy name is a football club director's.)

The first chance of the game was ours, in the third minute, but Vaesen, in the Huddersfield goal, made a good stop from Bull's close-in shot. In the 18th minute we fell behind, to a Dalton shot that was deflected off Muscat into our net. Wolves looked rattled as Town piled on the pressure. In the 28th minute, to the jeering delight of the home crowd, Steve Froggatt unintentionally sent Fernando sprawling on the ground – in a way, the confusion summed up our performance. But we came back into it: just on half-time the Wolves attack took the Town defence apart, David Connolly heading over the advancing Vaesen but, as he rounded the keeper, the ball raced away from him and over the end-line.

It was still 1–0 to Town at the interval but I was optimistic. In the corridor, heading for my half-time cuppa, I almost collided with Sir Jack of Molineux.

'What d'you think, sir?' I blurted out, astonished to find myself so close to the Saviour of the Wolves.

'We should've had that goal,' Sir Jack said, as if he were quite accustomed to being addressed in Huddersfield corridors by total strangers with Irish accents. Maybe millionaires are just like that.

We eventually got our goal but we had to wait until the 89th minute for it. As Vaesen came out, Robbie Keane coolly lobbed the ball over his head into the empty net. Robbie had done little in the game but we forgave him now, and we rejoiced with him as he performed his trademark cartwheel of celebration. As the Wolves end cheered, so the home crowd was stunned into silence. At least, I told myself, we're on the right end of these last-minute goals this weekend.

But we weren't. We were still digesting our last-gasp let-off as Town swept upfield and, as a back-pedalling Sedgley fumbled a headed ball into the path of Ben Thornley, the Huddersfield striker gratefully clipped the ball over Stowell into our net.

It was 2–1 to Town. In the 48th minute of the second half. Why was the old Celestial Director doing this to us? What had we done to deserve these last-minute hammer blows?

Even now, long after the event, I can still recall the terrible breathlessness of that moment, the sickening realisation of yet another needless loss that cannot be retrieved. I could no longer see the curved roofs of this beautiful stand soaring whitely against a backdrop of thick pine trees on the Yorkshire hills: I could see nothing except the injustice of this ending to a beautiful day in a beautiful place.

It was long after five when we came out of the stadium. The street wore that faintly sad look of all such places where crowds have milled and cheered and left behind them only their litter.

Captain Bird's-Eye was standing on the pavement, near the Wolves team coach.

'The luck wasn't with you today,' he said.

'Maybe we didn't deserve it,' I answered.

'They did their best,' the Captain said.

The anger and the frustration went out of me, standing there on the pavement outside the McAlpine, listening to this generous fellow who recognised his good fortune but refused to crow over it. The hills grew softer in the lowering sun: tomorrow that sun would rise again; tomorrow was another day. The heart was cut but no one had died. Football held more than goals at its lunatic heart: it held friendship too; a remembrance of hands clasped, of laughter shared. The soldiers at the front in the Great War knew that too, when they climbed out of their bloody trenches on that Christmas Day of long ago and laid down their arms to kick a football about on the scarred earth of no man's land. In their shared passion for the simple business of competitive play, those tired men might have found a simpler solution for their world's ills than blowing one another to smithereens; the generals knew that too and they feared it – mostly they feared that simple, ordinary men might discover on a rubble-strewn pitch that what they held in common was greater than any of their differences. The generals made sure that the football spontaneity of that wartime Christmas Day would never be repeated. The killing went on; the lucky ones, like Granda Garvey, ended up in wheelchairs in the far-flung towns of an empire whose days were numbered.

Captain Bird's-Eye of Huddersfield and Crewe, footballing acquaintance for a single, sunny afternoon in the West Riding, I salute you from Wolverhampton. Very likely, you will never read these words; very likely too, our paths will never cross again. Like football folk, we knew all that: we never even swapped names. No matter: you taught me something of grace and generosity and good humour that day in Yorkshire, and you are alive in these words.

7

Commandments of the CDF

We played Bury at home on 28 September but I have no recollection of that game whatsoever. The memorabilia of that football season assure me that I was there – Steve Corica looks back at me from the cover of the match programme; my own handwritten scribble on the team sheet reminds me that Fernando came on for the injured Simon Osborn in the 13th minute of the first half and that, five minutes from time, David Connolly was replaced by Michael Gilkes.

My own notes remind me of what I cannot recall:

6: Bull balloons sitter over bar from edge of square
25: Our best move – Robbie over – from edge of box

And further down:

43: Over PA: 'So-and-so please call home – your wife's in labour!'

Maybe (dare I say it?) we ourselves were labouring on the pitch but at least Bully delivered (ouch!) a goal with a headed bullet in the 21st minute . . . I know, because my notes tell me so, even if an amnesiac curtain has been drawn over my recollection of that afternoon. What I do recall is the collective sense of relief around Molineux: at last, on the final Saturday of September (but not the last game of September) we had gathered our first three-points result of the month.

Manager Mark McGhee must have shared our communal sense of relief. Alongside a photograph of McGhee in that morning's *Sports Argus* (an influential Midlands specialist sports newspaper) was the headline 'HEAD ON THE BLOCK'; the message was further sharpened by a cartoon of the bespectacled Mark kneeling with his head in the cut-out block while looking up (with understandable anxiety) at a rapidly descending, neck-seeking axe. In the streets and on the coaches there had long been rumblings of discontent with Mark's stewardship: as early as August, when we had played no more than a game or two, the newspaper vendor who sold me my *Express and Star* had assured me that 'McGhee would be gone by Christmas' – and he had spoken with such authority that I wondered if Sir Jack were numbered among his clients. The early September results must have caused Mark to finger his collar with not a little trepidation but the 1–0 win over Bury meant that, for the moment anyway, his neck was safe.

September, however, was still unfinished. There remained the Tuesday evening game on the 29th, against Queen's Park Rangers. There is nothing at all hazy about my recollection of this game. Rather, I recall only too clearly the frustration and the mounting anger of that Molineux evening.

On paper, QPR should have been a doddle for us. They hadn't won an away game for over a year. From nine outings in the present campaign, they had gathered a mere six points; only Tranmere ranked below them in the Division One table. Worst – or best – of all, the club seemed in disarray: just days before their visit to Wolverhampton their manager, Ray Harford, had walked out, leaving the team in the hands of caretaker Iain Dowie. All, surely, adding up to a scenario for a leisurely stroll in the park for our heroes in gold and black?

On that September evening the Celestial Director of Football was intent on reminding us of certain truths, for example:

1. Sod's law also applies in football.
2. Teams with caretaker managers are dangerous.
3. Bottom-of-the-table teams rouse compassion in Wolves' collective breast, as at Port Vale, earlier in the month.
4. Murphy's law also applies in football (cf. 1 above).
5. To win, you must score goals.
6. To not lose, you must stop the other fellows scoring goals.
7. The other fellows have a different script.

The CDF lost no time in ramming home to us these seven truths.

Less than two minutes into the game we were a goal down when Mike Sheron sidefooted the ball home from close range. Six minutes later it was 2–0 to QPR, Sheron again the scorer. A half-hour later I heard someone behind me in the Billy Wright stand roaring: 'Why don't you resign, McGhee!' Only a fabulous fingertap-over by Stowell in the 39th minute kept the score at 2–0 at half-time. Substitute Dominic Foley pulled a goal back for us 15 minutes from the end but, for the second time in a few days, Wolves were booed off the pitch by their own supporters. By then the rain had come, sleeting down on a disgruntled Molineux. Sometimes, I thought, driving home along the rain-slick Tettenhall Road, that old CDF laid on the stage effects just a bit too thick . . .

Only later that night, when I digested from Central TV the other results of the night, did I grasp the irony of it all. Sunderland had been held to a 2–2 draw at Norwich while Huddersfield, away to Stockport, had also been able to manage only a draw. Together they topped the table on 20 points – where we would have joined them had we managed a win in that last game of September. Instead, defeated, we remained on 17 points, and had slipped to 7th place. Birmingham had climbed two points above us; so too had Bolton, who had begun the month seven points and nine places below us. Ipswich too seemed to be working up a fine head of steam – their September record of three wins and a draw had yielded them a haul of ten points and taken them to within a point of us. Alongside such progress, our September harvest of only four points looked pitiful.

The race for the Premiership was well and truly on and we could not hide from ourselves the unhappy truth that already we were losing ground.

8

Getting a Life

The great Liverpool manager, Bill Shankly, has often been quoted as saying that football isn't a matter of life and death: it is, he said, much more important than that.

I think I understand what he meant – the feeling that every match-day Saturday is the hinge of your week, the day on which all the other days turn, in regret or exultation, with anticipation or foreboding. On match-day afternoons passion enflames existences that are otherwise mundane; ordinary lives are, for the span of a game, vested with the potential of worlds far greater than our own. Toolbox and keyboard are forgotten in the shared passion of a common cause; so are spouses, lovers, children – but soon enough, after the final whistle, life off the pitch comes elbowing its way into your bloodless battlefield, littering your patch of dreams with reminders of appointments unkept and bills unpaid and birthdays unremembered.

And yet it is off the pitch that we live our lives. In the end, football is *not* more important than life or death; rather it is what gives meaning to millions of lives.

Which means, of course, that it's rather a good idea to have a life.

My life, as I settled into Wolverhampton, revolved around the twin hubs of Saturday afternoon and Tuesday night; for the rest of the week I set about becoming familiar with my adopted town. Obvious foundations had to be laid, like locating a supermarket and a bank; a dentist and GP were also on my shopping list but, fortunately, in those early months I had no need of either. I haunted the library, searching for books on Wolves (a pathetic handful) and Billy Wright (a more pathetic total absence). I knelt in the lovely old redbrick Anglican church of St Peter in the heart of the town and in the less lovely Roman Catholic church just down the slope. I lingered with the *Express and Star* over tea and scones in Drucker's of Dudley Street and in Madame Cha-Cha's of King Street. I took to my heart the streets of this town, marvelling at the fabulous names – in what town are there streets more magically christened than Mitre Fold and Blossom Fold? Whisper them for yourself and in their exotic syllables you can glimpse the light of other times, of empurpled prelates parading through fields of springtime flowers.

I had come to this Black Country town intent on liking it, yet I soon realised that I was learning to love it; I had come here with the intention of going back to Galway after my football-book assignment had ended – but it took only months for me to realise that I might want never to leave this town. On a couple of occasions, half laughing, as if to pretend I wasn't being quite serious, I tried to tell one or two locals of my growing feelings for the town and I was astonished by their response: they seemed to be amazed that any outsider could see any loveliness in their town. And I told them what I have written here – about the quaint names, the broad, leafy thoroughfares to the west where I had chosen to live; the green spaciousness of West Park and the geese honking in the still evening air. Most of all, I told them about their own friendliness, their conviction that two words are always better than one, especially to a stranger in their midst; and I told them about the magic of seeing children and pensioners in Wolves' gear, not just on a match day, but on any common-or-garden wet Tuesday or windy Wednesday – yes, we have such days even here in the paradise of the Black Country – and I was humbled by their modesty, by their refusal to boast of their splendid town.

Even so, I needed something more than worshipful street-walking to fill the long gap from Saturday to Tuesday – and the even longer one from Tuesday back again to Saturday.

Wulfrun College was a handy, five-minute walk from my flat but, alas, they had no need of a well-qualified, experienced teacher of English to foreigners or of creative writing to would-be creators. It was the same story at the town's Adult Education Centre: more smiles and good chat and good-humoured courtesy but, alack, no timetable gaps for me to fill with my Irish enthusiasm.

Maybe that other Celestial Director – the one in charge of education – was trying to tell me something. Like, if there's no chance to teach, then maybe it's a good time to be taught.

The postman on Tettenhall Road must have been saying prayers for me. In answer to my phone calls, a small forest of postgraduate prospectuses came tumbling through my ground-floor letter box from colleges all over the English Midlands – Birmingham, Warwick, Staffordshire, Worcester and educational points further afield. I settled on two – Bretton Hall, part of the University of Leeds, because it offered a particular English course that interested me, and the University of Wolverhampton because – well, simply because it was Wolverhampton. Since the U of W, however, seemed to have an aversion to answering either letters or phone calls from scribbling Irishmen – it was the first and only discourtesy I encountered in my lovely town – my choice was necessarily narrowed to one.

Maybe footballers have gone to Spurs instead of Everton, or to Middlesbrough instead of Forest, for such simple reasons: somebody didn't return a call or acknowledge a letter. The silence from U of W was, in any case, a fortunate silence for me: it meant that, starting on the first Monday in October, the journey north from the Black Country to Yorkshire became a regular – and welcome – part of my week. I was, grey hairs and all, a registered MA student of Bretton Hall but, in a way, the course hardly seemed to matter: what mattered was that I had stumbled, almost blindly, into yet another happy band of like-minded students and teachers and that, week after week, I journeyed from one heartland to another.

9

The Word of God

On the Saturday before I made my first trip up to Bretton, Wolves were playing away to Crewe. The Alex are a small club, their neat, homely ground at Gresty Road having a capacity of no more than 6,000. The team sheets distributed to the press are handwritten, like the amateurish offerings of some church-based team run by a local enthusiast. Dario Gradi, MBE, is, of course, anything but amateurish: manager since 1983, he has sustained his tiny club at a high level through an unequalled youth academy and a shrewd approach to the business of buying and selling players. Even so, these Railwaymen should have provided an easy passage for Wolves: we were their betters, after all, in size, in wealth, in our fabled history. And despite our wretched September, we were ranked a dozen places above the Alex in the table: in ten games they had won only twice, gathering a mere ten points in the process. Even better, from our point of view, was their record of goals conceded – up to that point they had let in 20 goals as opposed to our Scrooge-like nine.

All in all, it looked like a pleasant outing for us. The run up the M6 to Crewe is a short one, but we pulled in, anyway, for our break: the pre-game coffee and analysis had become an essential part of our away-day liturgy. That morning our analysis was comfortable, optimistic. An about-to-be-out-of-contract Steve Froggatt had been sold for £1.9 million to Coventry (a transaction which would have pleased nobody at Molineux except the Board of Directors) but Steve Bull, I was able to assure Ray and Len, would definitely play against this leaky defence, despite predictions from all sides that our top-scorer would be out for knee surgery. Hadn't the great man told me so himself, just the day before, in the trophy-rich reception area of Molineux?

My historic dialogue with our living legend happened in this way: on Friday I'd called in to Molineux to leave our Galway local paper, the *Connacht Tribune*, at reception for Seamus Crowe, one of the club's young professionals. The paper was sent to me every week by my sister-in-law and, although I rarely read the paper when I lived in Galway, its arrival in Tettenhall Road had become one of the highlights of the week. I devoured it with relish; when I had done with it, it seemed only fair to pass it on to young Seamus. Discovering that a townsman of my own wore the old-gold shirt (although not yet for the First XI) seemed, in a small way, to legitimise my own addiction to an unseen Black Country club; what confirmed this footballing town-twinning was that Seamus had had trials with other and bigger clubs but had known, as soon as he saw Molineux, that this was where he wanted to pull his boots on. So, on that historic Friday, as I handed over my week-old copy of the *Connacht Tribune* to Barbara at the reception desk, I realised that it was indeed Steve Bull who was sitting alone on the coach, idly turning the pages of a magazine.

How d'you behave when you are up close to someone who has stepped off the pages of history? Here was a hero who wore the golden cloth of our dreams, but he was off-duty now, like some corporate executive in his dark business suit. Surely such a man is entitled to his privacy, without botheration from visiting Irishmen?

I was at the door, on my way out, when I realised I'd never forgive myself if I didn't open my mouth. I went back; I stood beside the magazine-covered coffee table.

'Steve?' I was scared too. 'Excuse me.'

'Aw' right, mate?'

'How're you feeling?' Deep, incisive questioning.

'Aw' right, mate.'

'How's the knee, Steve?'

I note the shaven head that has menaced defenders up and down the land but the expression is kind.

'Aw' right, mate, thanks.'

'And tomorrow?' Reckless now, pushing on. 'You'll hardly be playing?'

'I'll be playing tomorrow, mate.'

'But the surgery — ?'

'Next week, mate.' Did he grin or does memory deceive? 'I'll be playing tomorrow.'

I thanked him, wished him luck and withdrew. I started to breathe again when I was outside the door, leaning against the Billy Wright statue. With stuttering wings I had flown high and close to the god and my presumptuousness had been met with kindness.

And Bully would line out against the Railwaymen's creaky defence: it was just the ticket, we agreed, sipping our service-area coffee, to get our promotion drive back on the rails.

We arrived early in Crewe so I wandered off alone to have a look at the town — especially the railway station. I like stations. As a boy long ago in Galway I used to detour with my pals through the station there to the railway footpath that took us home to the barracks. We'd kneel on the mound of stones and press our ears close to the shiny metal to listen for the vibrant humming of an approaching train, and in my head I'd catch the songs of other towns, distant places. I can still dawdle with pleasure over a frothy cappuccino at Waterloo or Victoria and in the bustle of these great concourses and the PA announcements of yet more delays I can almost touch the days of boyhood and I can almost walk the streets of towns and cities I have never seen. I had thought that in Crewe Station I would see and smell and hear the sights and sounds of the four corners of Britain; that here at this railroad hub people would come parading not just from today but from an imperial yesterday through the open doors of my too-willing imagination.

Inside the glass front of the station a black hoarding walled off the past and present even from my fertile mind. Apart from a lone student-type stooped at the ticket window, the lobby was deserted. If this was the hub of the world, then the world no longer bothered to turn. Even the BR caff was closed. Or maybe the staff were just stuck on a delayed train . . .

But there was bursting life on the small, intimate streets surrounding Gresty Road. I stood in a shop doorway, sheltered against a biting wind, and I tucked with relish into well-browned chips smothered with salt and vinegar and in the noisy, good-humoured crowds milling towards the game I found the energy and the excitement that had been missing at the station. In these little redbrick streets where doors opened on to the footpath I could smell the metal polish on my grandmother's shiny doorknob and letter box and I had a sense of real lives lived and shoes polished and ties straightened. And scarves and colours donned: red and white, the colours of the Alex. They were on their toes, excited by the arrival of millionaire-Wolves, a scalp for the taking.

I sat among them inside the ground. It was a game that made you wonder how many chances we could fail to take. And chances aplenty we had, after an early spell of Crewe pressure that drew one brilliant tip-over save from Mike Stowell. It didn't seem to matter whose boot the chance fell to – Steve Bull, Carl Robinson or Robbie – all of them seemed strangely inept. (Muscat, at least, was true to form, getting himself a yellow card for a backhander into the face of a breakaway Shaun Smith). Carl's misses included a sitter early in the second half; Robbie could hardly manage to avoid the off-side trap, let alone take his chances when he did.

The unsatisfactory result of our trip to Gresty Road was a 0–0 draw.

Maybe it was a predictable outcome: we seemed unwilling, even afraid, to deliver the *coup de grâce* to bottom-of-the-table opposition like Vale, QPR and now Crewe. We made the journey home to Wolverhampton without our customary stop; I can't remember now, looking back, if Ray or Len was under domestic orders to be home early . . . what I do remember is that our morning-time cheer had evaporated in the wintry chill of Gresty Road. I remember, too, our unease about Bull – Steve had played, as he said he would, but he had been spectacularly ineffective and the concern now had to be that perhaps Steve had done needless damage to a knee that had already served (and suffered) with bravery and distinction through umpteen campaigns. None of us, however, fully realised quite how long it would be before Steve again pulled on the gold-and-black shirt.

Manager Mark McGhee was, apparently, afflicted with no such concerns. I kept a newspaper report of the game, a cutting which is at my elbow now as I write. The report concludes with a quote from Mark:

'I can't believe there's a manager in the Football League or the Premier League who doesn't want my job. I can't do anything about that,' McGhee said. 'But I've got it, at least until the end of the season.'

Mark should have known better than to tempt that old CDF.

Our game against Sheffield United the following Saturday was postponed, owing to international call-ups for the European Championship qualifiers. That day I took a trip to Ludlow. I wandered among the market stalls in the town square; I walked around the walls of the castle; I drank tea in a corner caff that had red formica-topped tables left over from the 1960s. I fiddled my way through the narrow streets and the long afternoon but, of course, what I yearned for was not to be found in that historic old town.

I wanted football. More specifically, I wanted to be at a Wolves game. The afternoon was a bleak glimpse of what my life would be when I returned to Galway after my season in the Black Country: no junkie ever stared with such shuddering knowledge into a long, fixless night as I did that wintry Saturday. It was dark when I left: the winding, hilly roads to Wolverhampton demanded my full concentration but still, at the back of my mind, I could sense a new dilemma articulating itself into life. It was no longer a case of when I went back to Ireland, but if . . .

On Monday morning I was on the road again, back up to Bretton Hall. I stayed the night in Barnsley, marvelling that such a lifeless town had been able to produce a team that had managed to win promotion to the Premiership – maybe they all went to bed early on Monday nights to conserve energy. Soon after Tuesday lectures ended, I was heading south again, homeward bound on the M1. It was a part of the week I would learn to fear and loathe – this long pull through the darkness towards the unseen lights of Tettenhall Road. I was wrecked when I got into the flat but at least I could enjoy the luxury of rising late the following morning . . .

I was having tea in front of the fire, wondering if I could work up the energy to take myself to bed, when the phone rang. It was my brother in Galway: my father had been taken to hospital and he was dying.

10

Journey to the Past

Next morning it was still dark when I nosed the old Kadett out on to the A41. Heavy rain lashed down all the way up to Chester where, just south of the city, I swung left and west towards Holyhead on the A55. Nursing the old car along the north coast of Wales, I was almost glad of the rain, drowning out the reason for this unscheduled journey. West of Conwy the rain stopped and exhaustion hit me: I pulled into the car-park of a Little Chef, angled my seat back and within seconds I was sound asleep. When I awoke, roused by a revving sports car, I was at first alarmed that I had slept too long but the dashboard clock showed that I had been out for no more than half an hour. Cold, stiff and bone-weary, I ate breakfast before pushing on westward along the coast. The bleak and beautiful landscape might have been lifted from the southern stretches of Connemara, to the west of Galway.

They'd been trying to reach me, my brother had told me, while I'd been away in Yorkshire; he'd been reluctant to leave such news on my answering machine. He didn't know how long my father had – a few days, a few weeks, maybe even a few months. The doctors couldn't – or wouldn't – say. What they did say, after his emergency re-admission to hospital, was that my father's cancer had returned. Three years previously, when he'd first complained of difficulty in speaking and swallowing, they'd found cancer in a large tumour on his thyroid gland. Chemotherapy and loving care had, apparently, gotten rid of the tumour and the cancer and had given back to my father a still-independent life. The cancer was back, but it was no longer a malignant tumour: in his ageing body it had metamorphosed into acute leukaemia. Despite the doctors' evasiveness, Jacky himself felt that our father didn't have a lot of time.

There was time to snooze again in the car, before we boarded the Stena-cat at Holyhead, but sleep refused to come now. My father was dying; what had been left unspoken between him and me would never now be spoken.

I was about eight years old when I stopped seeing my father as a safe place to shelter from the world. Up to that time he'd helped me occasionally with schoolwork; up to that time too I'd been a rather plump well-made little fellow who was good at school and happily engrossed in the communal life of the Married Quarters in the barracks. As I grew out of my baby-fat and into my own lankiness – and as I grew too into a wider knowledge of school and town – so did my perception of my father change. I became aware of the heavy, shadowed side of his nature and I flinched from its darkness.

But there was no escaping it.

That darkness spilled like septic rain over our house in the married quarters. He used to berate my mother for her poor management of the household. I was the eldest but I cowered under his anger, frightened and ashamed of my own fear, while my mother's eyes filled up with tears. All I knew in my boy's heart was that my mother baked sweeter apple-tarts and knitted better jumpers than any other mammy in the whole barracks . . . but I held my frightened tongue, terrified of the angry rain. I wanted to shout at him that there was nothing my mother could do about the gentle reminders from Egan's Grocery in town and Mr Duggan's shop out the road: she just didn't have enough money so what else could she do except buy the bread and jam and butter and tea and everything else on tick? There'd be no reminders at all from the shopkeepers, I wanted to yell at him, if you'd give her some extra money every Friday and not keep so much in the breast pocket of your tunic for spending in the mess on drink . . .

Drink and Fridays: they went together.

My mother got her army cheque on Friday mornings and used it for groceries and wool and bus fares. My father got paid on Friday mornings and gave some to my mother. The rest was kept folded in his tunic pocket for drink and cigarettes and horses. By Wednesday or Thursday the tunic pocket might be empty; sometimes my mother might be instructed to add a packet of fags to her slate-list for the shop.

Friday, however, was the weekly arrival of the horn of plenty. It was the night when, after tea at the oilcloth-covered table in the kitchen, still uniformed but capless and unbelted, he headed for the NCOs' mess in the big, grey-limestone building at the edge of the parade ground. It was the night, too, when I hoped I'd be asleep when he came back – I didn't want to be awake, in the big army bed in the room behind the kitchen, listening to his boozed complaints and my mother's tearful protests.

Christmas had its own special Guinness-sodden unloveliness. Many of the soldiers went 'on the tack' for six weeks or so before Christmas, leaving on the payroll each week an accumulating nest egg which they would draw on the last pay-day before the holiday. Some of the men used these savings to help pay for Santy and the other extras of the season; for others, like my father, the money was their personal ammunition to 'break out'.

'Breaking out' meant three or four Fridays coming one after another in the same week. 'Breaking out' meant tears and rage and despair in the night and my mother's face haggard in our sullen morning kitchen. On one Christmas Day we waited into the afternoon for our Christmas dinner, while my mother fretted over the now ready bird in the oven and the 'breaking out' went on breaking in the bowels of the mess.

It would never have entered my mother's mind to start without him. Maybe fear contributed to that, but mostly, I think, she simply worshipped him. My father was a handsome fellow, with a long, chiselled jaw and dark, straight hair above clear eyes and a strong nose. He was only a little over 5ft 8ins in height but he had the torso of a bullock and thighs and biceps that rippled with hard, blue-veined muscle. He was an intelligent man and a noted sportsman to boot: among the men of the Married Quarters his name and his face were the only ones ever to appear in the daily newspaper. You could read his name and look at his picture in the paper any old Monday after a Sunday hurling match. In 1953, when I was ten years old, I stood with my mother in Croke Park to watch him line out with the Galway hurling team in the All-Ireland final against Cork (the English equivalent would be to watch your dad playing in an FA Cup final at Wembley). My mother was thrilled and I was overwhelmed . . . but not with love. By then I had learned not to trust him. Too much Guinness had been pissed under too many bridges.

I sat near the front of the boat and watched Ireland loom towards us out of the blue afternoon. The crossing takes a little over an hour and a half. One hundred minutes to travel from one country to another. The journey from today to yesterday is even shorter. The past travels always on your shoulder.

I knew I shouldn't do it but I slapped Jacky anyway, across the face. My brother was 12, three years younger than me and forever making a pest of himself, losing my books, breaking my nibs and generally getting in my way. Jacky didn't cry: he rarely did – even then he was as tough as old army boots.

But I knew I was in trouble when I saw my father pushing his chair back from the tea table. He'd told us once to shut up before going back to his newspaper at the other end of the table, seemingly uninterested in our bickering. Now the folded paper was laid on the table, his army armchair skewed angrily back against the glass case. For a moment our kitchen seemed to hold its breath, as though my mother and the other children were afraid to breathe. I watched my father advance upon me as if he were moving in slow motion – the veins on his arms bulged below the rolled-up sleeves of his army shirt. I pushed my own chair back, trembling, and braced myself. I clenched my fists and made ready to defend myself.

He snorted derisively.

'You'll raise your fists to me, will you?' He feinted a blow to my midriff and as I dropped my hands I felt a stinging thump on the side of my head. 'You pup, you.'

And he struck me again. And again.

He went on cuffing me with both hands around my face and head. My sisters were weeping, my mother shouting. I hung there, trapped between chair and table while the beating and the shouting and the weeping went on. At length he stopped, pushing me away from him dismissively before going back to his chair and his paper.

In the frightened silence of our kitchen I could hear my own whipped whimpering. I felt the eyes of all of them on me and through my own blinded sobbing I could see what they saw: my pimpled face red and raw and streaked with tears and snot, my long skinny frame hanging like a broken reed over the end of the table.

'Go and wash your face, Kevin.'

My mother's words seemed to come as from a great distance. Still whimpering, I stumbled towards the bathroom; if I could not wash away my shame and snot, at least I could hide there.

Nobody spoke when I passed through the kitchen again, gathering up my books for evening study at school. By then we had left the married quarters, moving to another army house a couple of hundred yards from the barracks. I met no one as I cycled in the lee of the barracks wall and then along the unlighted line towards town. The darkness of the winter night was something to be grateful for.

I managed to sit, unweeping, through the two hours of study. Afterwards I stood with my best pal on the stone bridge at the end of the school street and I blurted out to him what had happened. I looked down over the bridge into the dark waters of the river while I spoke, as though my tale belonged to someone else. I told him I was never going home again and I heard him ask me, gingerly, what would I do then, and I didn't answer him. Even the dark river knew the answer, endlessly coursing towards the only home it could ever know. We lingered on the bridge, saying little, sharing the silence. Then he said he'd have to go, that he'd be in trouble if he got home late, and we said 'good luck' to each other and I swung my leg over the bike and I pedalled through the town towards home.

Not for weeks did I speak to my father. I saw him coming towards me one night, walking with my mother along Eglinton Street, and I stepped off the pavement and passed them by in silence. Long afterwards my mother's hurt expression stayed with me. She made overtures to me after that and, since I could never refuse her anything, I broke the silence with my father. Neither of us ever again referred to what had happened.

It took me over an hour to get through the choked streets of south Dublin from the ferry port to the open road west. Once there, the car seemed to perk up, like an old horse smelling again the fields of home. I took her gently, taking care even on the too-short stretch of motorway to hold her at seventy. The roads that she and I had travelled together were many and long; this, I had already decided, would be the last long journey we would make together.

I was the first of all my clan — Brophys or Garveys, in-laws or outlaws, generations living or buried — to go to university. Like all students from the town, I would live at home but I had won a clutch of scholarships to take care of fees and books and, maybe, even a little pocket money. I was proud of my achievement, and I knew that my mother was too.

That night in October 1961, the last night before I went up to sign on in the Aula Maxima at University College, she and I were chatting together in the sitting-room. It was the room where I studied; my books were stacked on one of the deep windowsills. Our talk was desultory but comfortable: whatever had to be said about the morrow had already been said and wondered over — and boasted about to the neighbours — more than once.

Tea, she said, she'd make us a cuppa. She ate nothing but the teapot was rarely given a rest. She was skinny as a rake but she was happy: I was starting college and my new baby sister was sound asleep upstairs. Through the half-open door I could hear the contented noises of kettle and lids and teapot as she went about making the tea.

My father came into the sitting-room. Our eyes met and I looked away from him.

'You're starting university tomorrow then?'

'Yes.' I waited: maybe, at last, the words of congratulation were about to come.

'Just don't think you're going to feather your nest here at our expense for the next few years.'

I could no longer hear the friendly sounds of my mother's tea-making from the kitchen.

'D'you hear me?'

I nodded, unable to meet his gaze.

When I lifted my eyes, after a long silence, the doorway was empty.

He was in the University Hospital, in a first-floor ward. My brother and his family shook hands with me and made space to let me closer to the corner bed. His eyes were huge, his jaw longer.

I took his hand in mine, pressed my fingers around his. It was too late now to learn kissing.

'I'm not going to make it this time, Kevin.' I knew the consultant had told him the score.

'I'd make you better if I could,' I said.

He said he couldn't hear me and I told him again.

'I know you would,' he said. We had learned to live with each other over the years. I used to take him to hurling matches and race meetings; sometimes we'd go drinking together.

The hospital rattled its way towards the end of visiting hours and the others left. I stayed, conscious of the nurses working their way towards us with night-time pills and smiles, but aware too of the long and tortured road that had taken us both to this point of parting. He dozed, opening his saucered eyes now and again as if wondering where he was; his breath whistled and wheezed through his open mouth. The hands that I had feared were pitiful now, exhausted on the hospital coverlet, their wounded veins darkened and swollen from the relentless, probing needles. When I turned my head, once, to look out at the uncurtained night, my own face, pale and haunted, stared back at me from the darkened window.

The following day I sat with him again through the long doldrums of the midday. He spoke but little. Sometimes he spoke in his dreaming sleep, but the words were broken too, beyond my comprehension.

Sometimes the hands fluttered from the bed, roused by his dreams; once, he lifted his right hand and pointed with one definite finger into the hospital air, or some other air, some other place, wherever his fragmented dreams were taking him. Old friends, some older than he was, began to arrive as the afternoon wore on; some of them, I knew, were saying their goodbyes to him so I left them to it and I wandered through the streets of my home town but the old familiar paths seemed strange to me, as though I had lost my way.

There was no obvious change in him the next day. He spooned a little yoghurt; he sucked at some vitamin drink through a straw. I watched the motions of the living and I watched me watching him. How can we lie there and not go out of our minds, knowing that the grave yawns for us? And how can we sit there, uttering our trite words of encouragement, knowing that neither straw nor spoon can close that gaping hole in the waiting earth? Is this why at the end, we dream of all our yesterdays – to shut out the spectre of the morrow? As if we might live again the days that are gone, but this time make them sweeter?

He was sleeping on the last afternoon that I saw him. He opened his eyes and seemed surprised to see me, sitting there beside the bed.

'I'm sorry, Kevin.' I watched him blink, his eyes casting about for signposts. 'I was dreaming.'

'What were you dreaming about?'

His eyes looked past me.

'I was dreaming about fields.'

'What kind of fields were you dreaming about?' I leaned closer. 'Dad?'

He was sleeping again, but it didn't matter. His words were an intimacy between us, a glimpse of a private world that, all his life, he had seemed afraid to uncurtain, at least to me.

Some time later, when I was making ready to leave, he wakened again.

'I have to go,' I said. 'I'm catching the train to Dublin and then flying out tonight.'

'Back to Wolverhampton?'

'Yes.'

We shook hands and, for a moment, his fingers tightened around mine.

'Safe journey,' he said.

I left him then. I had my own promises to keep, my own fields for dreaming. There was nothing more I could do here, no way of telling how long it would be before my father made his own final departure.

My son met me at Heuston Station in Dublin. There was time enough for him to take me to his house in Glasnevin and to meet again the two young men he shared the house with. There was time for coffee and time for these young fellows to tease me, gently, about Wolves' familiar stumbling progress. Afterwards, Adam drove me to the airport and I let go of the day, giving myself into my son's hands as he powered the shiny, new, company Mondeo along the motorway.

On the pavement outside Departures we hugged each other goodbye.

'I'll drive down to see Granda tomorrow,' he said. 'The girls are coming with me.'

'I'll be in Portsmouth myself.'

'Best of luck,' he grinned. 'You're going to need it.'

11

A Deep Ocean of Baloney

We didn't have any luck at Portsmouth. The day seemed to promise it – bright, hard, the motorways clear and open from the Black Country to the south coast. Ray and Len had collected me early that morning; I was tired after the trip to Ireland but relieved, too, to be back on my personal odyssey. I was looking forward to seeing Portsmouth. Like Wolves, Pompey had a past that was greater than their present: older-timers than myself could still recall the 1939 FA Cup final when a hotly fancied Wolves side disintegrated to Portsmouth, losing 4–1 at Wembley.

I saw little of Portsmouth. We entered the city along a broad thoroughfare and eventually found parking in a cramped, residential street. We then entered Tratton Park and we stayed put.

The game was littered with the inescapable irony of football. Steve Claridge had left Molineux, returning home to the south coast and lining out with Pompey. Inevitably, it was Claridge who 'won' the decisive penalty in the 20th minute of the second half. After a scoreless first half, Wolves were dominating the play but, when Claridge was adjudged to have been up-ended in the box by Curle, our dominance hardly seemed to matter. The referee dosed our wound with salt by sending Curle off before the penalty was taken. Allan McLoughlin added the poisonous irony by converting the penalty — the same Allan McLoughlin whose beautifully struck equaliser against Northern Ireland a couple of years earlier had sent the Republic of Ireland to the World Cup finals in the USA. The hero in the green had become a villain in the blue of Pompey.

We tried after that but our luck was out. So was Bull; so was Robbie. Without them we could not breach the Pompey defence.

In the North Atlantic, in 1912, the *Titanic* was fatally breached by a giant iceberg. In 1998, James Cameron's movie of the same name made sure that only Martians and, maybe, deaf-blind hermits didn't know about the ship's relegation to the lowest depths. You couldn't escape the wretched thing — posters loomed at you from billboards and magazines, the cloying theme song assaulted your eardrums on every radio and television station. The company of a female friend had forced me to sit through the entire fourteen hours of the movie soon after its release; I survived the experience, but with an ill grace. I like my characters rounded, my narrative credible, my dialogue realistic. At least, I comforted myself, I wouldn't have to sit through the whole nineteen hours of it again.

The Wolves Travel Club had other ideas. The supporters' coach was barely out of Wolverhampton when I realised what kind of voyage lay ahead. It was early on the afternoon of Tuesday, 17 October, three days after the defeat at Portsmouth; we were *en route* to Crystal Palace in south London. The steward was fiddling with the controls of the video machine at the front of the coach; only as the white diagonal streaks on the screen defined themselves into pictures did I realise that I was doomed.

There's nowhere to hide on a coach — although I did toy with the idea of spending the journey in the lavatory. The puerile script and the cardboard characterisation infuriated me; I understood, too late, the real benefit of travelling with a private stereo and giant earphones.

For once, I was at odds with my fellow fans. When I looked around, they were intent on the small screen.

I contented myself with scribbling down a few of the more choice lines:

Jack Dawson (artist extraordinaire): 'Look at his [Picasso's] *use of colour*'
Young Rose (art student extraordinaire): '*Isn't it extraordinary!*'

On my lap rested our Wolves fanzine but editor Charles Ross could never have produced such *A Load of Bull* as the screen did. It got better. In my notebook I recorded:

Old Rose: '*A woman's heart is a deep ocean of secrets.*'

The coach was not equipped with sick bags.

★

Our own ship started to founder after 40 minutes. Although still without Bull and Robbie, we were holding our own against a Palace side that might have lined out for the League of Nations – Sun Jihai and Fan Zhiji are Chinese, Nicky Rizzo is Australian, Attilio Lombardo is Italian while Matthias Svensson is from Sweden. On the bench for Venables' multinational Eagles was Sasa Curcic of Yugoslavia. In the 40th minute of the first half we cracked – Craig Moore got a boot to Rizzo's corner, the ball was in the roof of the net and we were, yet again, a goal down. We held Palace to a single goal until half-time but Wolves seemed devoid of goal-scoring ideas of their own. And what, you had to ask yourself, could David Connolly, tireless but also heightless, achieve up front on his own?

Our resistance in the second half didn't last long. After six minutes Stowell brilliantly saved a penalty but, from the corner that followed immediately, Lombardo sent a lovely, looping header into the corner of our net. You didn't have to be a mind-reader to understand Stowell's fist-swinging frustration and anger.

Of all people, it was defender Steve Sedgley who got us back into the game, with a downward-headed goal from a Corica cross. We huffed and puffed after that but it was Palace who managed to score next: Curcic, from a well-worked free kick, sent the ball low into the corner, leaving Stowell stranded.

At which point, furious and frustrated with Wolves, *Titanic* and creation in general, I stormed out of my seat to have a pee. Or something. Anything except to watch my lovely team go down the pan in another game they could have won. I was in the loo at the top of the stand washing my hands when I heard the cheering; by the time I rushed out, Palace were kicking off from the centre circle. Carried away, perhaps, by scoring his first-ever goal for Wolves, Sedgley had decided to score again – this time (so my neighbours told me) with his boot from close in. It was 3–2 now, but time had run out for us, the gaping hole below our waterline too great to be plugged.

Our journey home from London was, at least, *Titanic*-free, but it was a comfortless journey through the darkness. For the first time since our brief golden summer of August we had scored two goals in a league game . . . but we had still lost. From our previous four games – against QPR, Crewe, Portsmouth and Palace – we had taken only a single point, and that from our scoreless draw with lowly Crewe. Ahead of us, on the Saturday, lay what the commentators would call a 'tricky' home tie against Grimsby. I looked out at the dark night sliding by and puzzled over the extraordinary collapse in our fortunes: Mark McGhee, I figured, was probably puzzling over it too.

The possible 'trickiness' of the game was due to the presence of Alan Buckley as manager of Grimsby. A couple of seasons before, Buckley, then manager of West Brom, had seen his side go down 2–0 at Molineux; that Black Country derby defeat had signalled the end of Buckley's tenure as manager at the Hawthorns. On that morning of the Grimsby game, in a table headed by Huddersfield on 27 points, Buckley's team, on 22 points, stood an astonishing ten places – although only four points – above us. It was a day for settling scores, for healing wounded pride.

It was also my personal day for feeling one degree under: my head ached and my nose felt as soggy as the pitch looked. Personal colds and sodden surfaces were well and truly forgotten, however, when Irishman Dominic Foley lashed a rebound off the Grimsby post into the net to put us a goal in front. Fourteen minutes later it was 2–0: Richards was taken down in the Grimsby area and Curle sent Davison the wrong way with the penalty kick. Luck, woodwork and some dogged defending by Grimsby kept the score at 2–0 to the final whistle. By then the Wolves fans were in full and raucous voice, taunting the Grimsby manager: my neighbours, straining like myself to make out the chanted words, were unsure whether the Molineux refrain was:

(a) *Alan Buckley's fucking ugly*

or

(b) *Alan Buckley's fucked it up again*

Either way, the Grimsby boss and his squad hit the road out of Wolverhampton with unbecoming haste, not even bothering to give the customary post-match press conference. The win lifted us – just – out of the bottom half of the table. Whether it would be enough to save Mark McGhee's job was questionable. Ominously, the attendance of 18,480 was the lowest for a Saturday league game at Molineux since 1993.

As Wolves pulled themselves back, my father inched his way towards the edge. I called my brother in Galway most nights, keeping abreast of the situation at the hospital. Three days after the Grimsby game, Jacky phoned to say that my father had been transferred to the hospice and was now nearing the end. I rang Aer Lingus to book a flight out of Birmingham to Shannon the next day. I was lying awake, around five o'clock in the morning, when the phone rang. I knew it would be Jacky, and I knew what he was going to tell me.

12

Gunfire in the Rain

The rain never stopped on that last Saturday in October when we buried my father. The army took charge. They draped his coffin in the Tricolour of Ireland and stationed it before the altar of the tiny garrison church where, as a boy, I had served mass for so many years. Men and women from civvy street knelt among the uniforms in the crowded pews and huddled under umbrellas on the pathway and on the road, but you could not doubt that this was a day when soldiers were saying goodbye to one of their own. Uniformed NCOs slow-marched through the chapel on either side of the coffin and stowed it in the black hearse for its slow and final journey to the cemetery. The same NCOs shouldered it among the crowded headstones to its last resting place.

My son and my daughters pressed close to me as the soldiers took the strain of the ropes and lowered the coffin into the wet earth where, over 20 years ago on a sunny day in March, we had laid my mother. The priest recited a decade of the rosary and splashed holy water into the open grave; he sprinkled a handful of sodden clay on the coffin. We wept and blew our noses and huddled together under our brollies and the endless rain covered the town and the sea and the hills across the bay with a curtain of darkest grey.

The voice of the sergeant-major came low and almost apologetically across the terraces of graves and the firing party raised their weapons to their shoulders, and we heard another command in Irish, low as the first, and then the volley of shots crackled in the sodden skies. Three times they fired; three times I felt my daughters flinch beside me.

I had not noticed the bugler until then. He stood a little distance from us on a small rise in the ground, green-caped against the rain, his bugle in his hand; beside him the drummer was ready, his kettledrum skirted now with graveyard black. In that rain-lashed cemetery on the hill above Galway Bay the bugler began to blow the 'Last Post'. It is the saddest melody in all the world, its long and mournful notes heavy with the lost years of the lost young of all the wars of the world. They played *reveille* then, the drummer tapping his muffled rhythm, as though by this brisk optimism they might convince us of the truth of final resurrection. The bugler ended alone, bringing us back to the reality of the wet earth and the dripping umbrellas and our dead father. It's the way of armies everywhere: they function by the organised extraction of emotion from their uniformed members and yet, more even than churches, they tear human hearts apart with the raw power of their liturgies.

The soldiers bent to lift in unison the door-sized board that would cover, temporarily, the open grave. As they shuffled, stooped and burdened, searching for solid footing on the greasy edges, I knew, finally and inescapably, the truth of my own loss: I had lost my father a long, long time ago, long before this rainswept Saturday. As a boy, I had shrunk in the withholding of his praise; as a man, I had learned to shrug my shoulders and pretend to ignore the unopened mouth. For most of his life, my father had been an imprudent man: when he had retired from the army he had been obliged to vacate his army house and would have had to settle for corporation housing had I not bought him a home to live in. He lived there for almost 20 years; it used to hurt that he never once said thank you. He could take what I offered and make me feel as if he had done me a favour.

On that rain-lashed hillside above the bay I began to realise another truth: that all my life, especially since my mother's death, I had been searching for my safe place, a place where you belonged, a place where somebody or something mothered you and fathered you. It was as if I could see, through the blinding rain, all the way back to that 1950s kitchen in the married quarters, when I had been safe and sure of my own place in the scheme of things. I could never go back to that time but I could seek again some of the touchstones of that lost world. My lovely Wolves were a part of it – I could see that now, through the sheeting rain, reflected back at me from the burnished handles and polished wood of my father's coffin.

After the graveyard ceremony the army had laid on a buffet reception in the NCOs' mess inside the barracks. Hundreds of men, women and children tucked into platefuls of snacks and sandwiches and warmed themselves with tea and coffee. The bar was opened; it did a brisk trade. The insistence of the living flesh banished again those brief intimations of mortality to the graveyard on the hill.

At around half past four that afternoon I left the heaving throng in the bar and found a TV in a corner of a quieter room. My son got it going; he left the sound off but we could imagine the clacking and clicking of the teleprinter as the BBC football results came in. A bunch of nieces and nephews and their pals were sprawled on chairs about the room, glasses in their hands; they knew about my Wolverhampton adventure; some of them seemed not unimpressed by my lunacy.

Our result came up at last on the screen: 1–1 against Barnsley. Not so bad, one of the young ones said, against a team from last year's Premiership. No, I agreed, not so bad – but my sodden brain still registered the information that we had taken the lead as early as the fifth minute, from a Muscat penalty, and still managed to lose two points.

I drifted back to the other room, getting ready to leave. A distant cousin, home from England and armed with a pint of Guinness, shouted at me above the hubbub, wanting to know how Wolves had done.

'One-all,' I told him, 'against Barnsley.'

'Were Wolves away?' he wanted to know.

'No,' I heard myself say, 'we were at home.'

13

A Farewell to Arms

Two weeks were to pass before I would see my Wolves play again.

On the Monday after my father's funeral I took the train to Dublin, flying on that night to Birmingham. I spent the night in my flat in Wolverhampton, sorting out shirts and socks and teaching materials; next morning I was back again at Birmingham Airport, bound, this time, for Düsseldorf, and then on by road to Langscheid in Germany's Sauerland.

Had I been asked, in the departure lounge at Birmingham, why I had agreed at such short notice to accept the two-week teaching assignment, I would have hummed and hawed, hardly able to read my own mind. The phone call from the school on the morning of the funeral had put me on the spot: they needed to know then and there if they should send a driver to collect me at Düsseldorf Airport. Under pressure, torn between past and present, between Galway and Wolverhampton I had said yes, without knowing why I did. Sometimes, your heart is the only voice worth listening to.

I had taught in Langscheid before, and had learned to love both the gentle sleepiness of the town and the gregarious routine of the school. The students are mostly working professionals on release from multinational corporations such as Ford, Mercedes and Bayer; students and teachers live together under the same roof for the duration of these intensive English-language courses. You work hard on these courses but there's good fun, too, especially in the evenings, when you have to organise your own entertainment – singsongs, readings, storytellings, or just having a jar and a chat. The teaching and the human contact soothed me, easing me away from the pain of the past, readying me for my return to the Black

Country. The empty flat that awaited me was, to be sure, at the heart of the Tettenhall Road's leafy, suburban elegance but, when all was said and done, it was still empty. For a while at least, I needed voices around me, and laughter, and a breakfast table that was not solitary.

In the hour between the end of class and the serving of dinner, there was time to be alone. Sometimes my evening walk took me through the nearly deserted streets of the darkening town, sometimes along the path that ran alongside the great reservoir. It was to the reservoir path that I took myself on the evening of 11 November: Armistice Day. In the amber light of the street lamps I could make out the faces of an elderly German couple out for their evening constitutional.

'*Guten Abend*,' I said, using up some 20 per cent of my entire German vocabulary.

'*Guten Abend*.' The man nodded, the woman smiled, as they passed me.

I lingered a while, following their purposeful progress until they stepped out of the light and the darkness swallowed them. By now, night had fallen, hiding the water and the forests and the surrounding hills. Yet the night was not truly dark: hundreds, maybe thousands, of lights were scattered on all of the hills around me; on the road above the reservoir I could see the moving headbeams of cars scything the darkness as they hurried towards the lights on those hills. *Guten Abend.* Hang up your coat. Put away your briefcase. Sit down to eat. How was it that, twice in this century, these ordinary folk who nodded and smiled at strangers in the evening, had gone to bloody war? From the hills I sensed the beat of drums, the crack of rifles, the dying echo of a bugle in the night; voices long dead whispered of the daftness of it all. I was sprung from the seed of soldiers but their genes had given me no taste for the madness of war. Or maybe that *was* the legacy of Lucan Street: that war is madness. Better to find a football and confine your war-whoops to a playing pitch. Maybe, in the 80 years since the Great War had ended, we had learned just a little.

Ian Willars, sports writer with the Birmingham *Evening Mail* and known to his peers as 'the Duke', had promised, with ducal largesse, to keep me up to date with Wolverhampton developments while I was away in Germany.

Ian was as good as his word: reports and comment from the *Mail* were coughed out of the fax machine in Langscheid with welcome regularity. The school secretaries, with fine Teutonic politeness, kept to themselves their opinion of their Irish English-teacher who was the recipient of these communications from the English Midlands: they handed me the reports, they smiled, they said, 'Is everything okay?'

It was and it wasn't.

On the Tuesday that I flew out of Birmingham, Wolves travelled to Ipswich and were soundly beaten 2–0. 'SHOT-SHY WOLVES ATTACK LACKING BITE' was the headline over Ian's report on the match. Bull's absence was compounded by Robbie Keane's injury; in the absence of both, Mark McGhee had brought in Guy Whittingham on loan from Sheffield Wednesday. Obviously the solution didn't fit the problem. And the blade had been unsheathed again: 'AXE HANGING OVER MCGHEE' read the headline on a piece from the *Evening Mail* which Ian faxed that evening.

In a short, accompanying note Ian wrote: 'Sadly I have to report that Saturday's game at Bristol could be Mark's last at Wolves – if they don't win.'

The Duke, in fact, was being unduly optimistic.

On the following day the board of Wolves finally swung the long-threatened axe: McGhee was sacked – 'although the official line was that he had left by mutual agreement' (*Birmingham Post*). It was a painful ending to a Molineux posting that had at first been welcomed by the Wolves' faithful. McGhee had begun his managerial career in 1991 at lowly Reading, guiding them to the verge of promotion to the top flight; in 1994 he took over at freefalling Leicester but had failed to prevent their drop out of the Premiership. The following year he had walked out on Leicester to take over a Wolves team that seemed destined, with Sir Jack Hayward's loot, for promotion aboard the Premiership gravy train. Three seasons later that destiny remained unfulfilled and McGhee was gone. I had met him once, for a pleasant chat at Wolves' training ground, on a bright morning in late September when we were well into our bad run and had tumbled a fair way down the table. He came across to me, sitting on that bench on the lawn of that tennis club, as an articulate, intelligent man; it was impossible to disagree with his comments about the misfortunes of injuries and last minute goals, such as those we had given away against Sunderland and Huddersfield.

In the end, time and fans' patience (the board's too) ran out for Mark McGhee.

The manager was dead: long live the manager.

McGhee's assistant, Colin Lee, was given the caretaker job.

Colin took Wolves to Bristol for his first game in charge. There, in full accord with the laws of football daftness, Wolves hammered City 6–1. David Connolly finally broke his duck and then, to nobody's surprise, went on to score three more. Whittingham and Robinson scored the other two for our rampaging Wolves.

Our German secretaries never even raised a perfect eyebrow when I danced a little jig around the school reception area, clutching Ian's fax to my singing heart.

I did a reprise on Wednesday morning, when Ian's report of our home game against Sheffield came through. The report was headed: 'TWO OUT OF TWO FOR LEE'S WOLVES'. A goal down at half-time, we had fought back after the break with a 49th-minute equaliser from Connolly and then, four minutes from time, Robinson's right-footed winner.

Two wins under Colin had taken us back to the fringe of the play-off positions. We were in seventh place but Bradford, in sixth, had only the same number of points (28). Above us were Sunderland (37 points), Ipswich and Birmingham (both 32), Watford (31) and Huddersfield (29).

'It's good news?' Petra asked me, when I had finished my personal *Riverdance* around reception.

'We're on the road back,' I told her. I felt like kissing her but she *was* the school boss and I hadn't been paid yet. 'Definitely,' I beamed, 'we're on the road back.'

And it was time, I knew, for me to be on that road also.

14

On the Road Again

Classes in Langscheid ended at midday on Friday, 13 November. Lorcan Flynn, German-based, Irish-born teacher and storyteller, had offered to drive me from the school to Düsseldorf Airport. He kidded me about travelling on such an ominous date but my optimism put me beyond the reach of such banter: Ian's dispatches from the home front clearly showed that our luck had turned. Germany had worked its post-funeral healing, filling my days with busy-ness and congenial company, but now I wanted to be home again, back in the middle of the authentic action. When the BA flight landed in the darkness at Birmingham, I hurried through the airport – I had nothing to declare except my pleasure at being back.

I slept only fitfully that night but I was ready and waiting when Ray arrived at the flat early the next morning. Ahead of us lay the long road to Norwich. We picked Len up in Birmingham, where he'd been presenting an early morning radio programme, and headed south-east along the M6. We left the motorway to join the A14, driving east through cold sunshine, then swinging south-east again below Huntingdon, skirting the unseen spires of Cambridge, to the south, before we swung north-east, bypassing Newmarket, sensing journey's end as we joined the A11. It was a journey to remember, cutting a swathe through the green flatlands of central England. I was glad to be back again on my pilgrimage. The sun was shining, we had a couple of victories under our belt and we were able to convince ourselves that the last corner had been turned. I wasn't alone in my optimism: I could read it in the bright-eyed faces of the gold-shirted fans that I chatted to in the Burger King where we pulled in for our coffee. That morning, Norwich stood just below us in the table, on 28 points, the same as ourselves. They also had two games in hand but everybody knew that that wasn't the same thing as having points in hand.

By the end of an afternoon that had turned bitterly cold, nothing would have changed about our respective league table positions. The result was a 0–0 draw but that goalless scoreline gives no idea of the passion aroused that Saturday, both on and off the pitch at Carrow Road.

The early pressure came from Norwich, Stowell just managing to push Eadie's low shot around the post in the eighth minute. Eight minutes later, from a corner, Mackay's header went mercifully over the bar. With just under half an hour played, Stowell fumbled a ball that was going wide, needlessly giving away a corner; when the high corner came in, our keeper fumbled it again but the ensuing scramble came to nothing. Four minutes after that, Iwan Roberts just failed to get on the end of a low cross and the ball went safely wide.

It was the kind of palpitating homecoming I hadn't envisaged but at least we survived the first half on level terms.

Three minutes into the second half came the game's defining incident. Lee Naylor was sent to the ground on the far touchline. Matt Jackson, the Norwich captain, was in the act of stepping over Naylor's fallen body when Lee started to rise; Jackson put his already raised foot on Lee's back and stepped on him and over him. Lee Naylor collapsed again on to the pitch. The referee blew his whistle, waved his red card at Jackson and Norwich were suddenly minus their captain.

To say that the home fans were incensed is to give no idea of the venom that now spilled from the stands of Carrow Road. After the ritual, chanted denunciation of the referee's sexual practices, the home crowd turned on Naylor with singular vengeance. The stadium became a cauldron of booing and jeering every time he touched the ball. The relentless pressure told. For the rest of the game Naylor was a passenger on the left wing. His every touch went wrong, his every pass astray – and every mistake was jeered all over again by the Carrow Road choir. I wondered why our manager left Naylor on the field: after the game he would say that youngsters like Lee Naylor had to learn to cope with all kinds of pressure and he hoped Lee had learned something from the experience.

Norwich's ten men held our ten (plus Naylor) at bay for the rest of the game. Robbie Keane came on, 13 minutes from the end, replacing Guy Whittingham; Robbie's first appearance since the Crewe game was loudly welcomed by our travelling supporters but he was obviously still not match-fit and the Norwich defence held firm. They might even have nicked it, just before the end, when Eadie crossed from the left but Iwan Roberts just failed to connect. At the post-match press conference, Bruce Rioch, the Norwich manager, said that he felt Wolves would be less pleased than he was with taking a point from the game.

Bruce would sing a different tune three weeks later, when Norwich came to Molineux, but before that we had to face Bolton Wanderers – and also a couple of explosive local derbies.

15

Local Derbies: You Win Some . . .

The first of these derbies was against Birmingham. In the week before that game, however, came the notorious *Guardian* incident, which almost resulted in Wolverhampton breaking off diplomatic relations with the newspaper.

On 18 November, *The Guardian* carried an advertisement promoting its own graduate jobs supplement. What roused Black Country ire was the headline on the advert: 'HAVE YOU GOT LESS CHANCE OF PROMOTION THAN WOLVES?' Those of us who knew better could recognise at once the glib hand of some poncey executive who probably held a season ticket for Stamford Bridge, but local pride still demanded an official response. It was delivered with the swiftness of a Bully strike.

Local MP, Dennis Turner, was quoted thus in the *Express and Star*: 'This is absolutely disgraceful. It is an absolutely outrageous slur on our beautiful town and our beautiful team.' Hear, hear.

Borough mayor Mrs Gwen Stafford Good said: 'I think there will always be somebody who is outside Wolverhampton and who can't understand us. We know how good Wolverhampton is and we know how good Wolves are.' And so say all of us.

It was left to Charles Ross, editor of *A Load of Bull*, to deliver the *coup de grâce* to the snivelling Chelsea-type who dreamed up the slur-laden advert: 'People in education have a sense of history and Wolves is one of the most romantic clubs, regardless of status, and any well-rounded graduate will know that.' A man after my own heart.

Whosoever cannot understand the indignant passions fired up by the incident has never dreamed a dream; he is, like the man that hath not music in him (or her), fit only for treasons, stratagems and spoils. Even so, we are forgiving folk in the Black Country: the sale of *The Guardian* was not forbidden thereafter in Wolverhampton. For myself, I went on buying the paper but, for three days, with impeccable Irish logic, I refused to read it.

★

The Sunday of our game against Birmingham City was a bitter, wintry day. It was a one o'clock kick-off but, even before the match started, the floodlights were on, pale under the grey, midday sky. I felt I was truly home again, walking past Billy's statue, the great man himself caught in mid-stride, eternally leading us towards the promised Premiership land. It was my first home game since the 1–0 victory over Grimsby.

Wolfie too was back, clowning about on the Molineux pitch: he'd been conspicuously absent the week before at Norwich, following his over-exuberant horseplay with the piggies of Bristol. Television and the national press had picked up on these animal antics: I'd already had a look at the newspaper clippings that had been saved for me while I'd been away in Germany.

On a Friday night in August, after we'd beaten Watford at Vicarage Road, I'd had a brief word with the occupant of the Wolfie costume; I knew he wasn't old enough to realise the significance of the date of today's game against the Blues. It was 22 November. Thirty-five years before, on the same date, John F. Kennedy had been killed in Dallas by an assassin's bullet. I didn't realise, watching the teams run out onto the pitch, that 22 November 1998 was also about to become a major landmark in my personal list of never-to-be-forgotten dates.

The first few minutes of the match made me think we were in for a right royal hammering. From the kick-off, Birmingham forced a corner. For the next three minutes I couldn't be sure if the panic among our supporters was greater than the panic among our players: for second after heart-stopping second we were pinned back in our own box and subjected to relentless pressure by a confident Blues team that seemed set on reminding us that they were fourth in the table, three places and three points above us. Mercifully, in the fourth minute the siege was lifted, Wolves charged upfield and, at the end of a sweeping cross-field movement, Kevin Muscat volleyed over the bar. Wolves had taken the initiative now: for the next five minutes they played the best football I'd seen that season. The Blues came back into it, of course: Trevor Francis's team didn't owe their lofty position to mere chance. The game crackled from end to end but overall I felt we had the edge.

Then, in the 21st minute, our fans were silenced. Furlong, standing in front of goal, took a low cross from the right wing, swivelled to steal a little space for himself and, before you could say Trevor Francis, he'd drilled the ball low into our net. The Blues' fans were in full voice in the lower deck of the John Ireland stand. I remembered it was Sunday; I wondered if we ought to start praying.

Muscat might have been thinking the same thing. As Wolves, still a goal down, ran out onto the pitch for the second half, I noticed the Australian stoop in mid-stride to touch the Molineux grass before blessing himself with the same hand. His gesture took me back to the seashore of my boyhood in Galway: I'd learned the same habit there, splashing my way into the summer sea − you crossed yourself with fingers that had touched the sea and you murmured the old words that would ensure deliverance from the deep. Or from defeat.

That deliverance came in the fourth minute after half-time when Robbie Keane came off the bench, where he'd been waiting alongside Neil Emblen and our new German signing, Robert Niestroj. The roar of delight that greeted Robbie's arrival changed to cries of concern when, barely on to the pitch, he was felled near the far touchline. Concern became panic when the stretcher was brought on: Robbie hadn't started a game since Crewe and Steve Bull was fast becoming a mere goal-scoring memory . . . Another roar, this time of relief, signalled the Keane-less departure of the stretcher-bearers; our boy wonder was okay. His effect upon the Birmingham defence was immediate: high up in the Billy Wright stand I fancied I could smell the panic among the Blues defenders every time our Robbie touched the ball.

Twenty-six minutes into the half, Lee Naylor slotted home his first goal of the season to put us on level terms. The manager, it seemed, had been right after Norwich: maybe Lee had been fired up, not broken, by the stick he'd taken at Carrow Road. Eight minutes later Robbie flicked the ball to Carl Robinson and Carl sent a glorious strike high into the Birmingham net. Now the stadium was ecstatic: 'We've got the Blues on the run' was the refrain that resounded to the November sky.

Birmingham proceeded to throw everything at us in a desperate search for an equaliser − the kitchen sink, Peter Ndlovu, the sitting-room suite and Paul Furlong – everything was now hurled against our goalmouth in a grandstand finish.

But the day was ours. Almost on the stroke of full-time, Wolves broke out and Carl Robinson, from the edge of the penalty area, lifted a beautiful, looping shot over Poole's head dropping low into the Blue's net.

A 3–1 victory after being 1–0 down: what more could you ask for? The result had also lifted us into a play-off position, behind Sunderland, Watford, Ipswich and Sheffield. Wolves were on the move; lesser creatures should beware. Bring on the Baggies.

I doubt if any youngster has ever fallen in love with West Brom because of their nickname. How could you grow starry-eyed over an outfit called 'the Baggies'? Baggy what? Baggy shorts? Under their backsides? Around their knees? Around their ankles? Or shirts around their midriffs? That nickname could never have whispered in my ear in our long-ago kitchen in the married quarters. Maybe, even then, in that disappeared household, I was in love with words and dreams and love itself. In my boy's mind I heard echoes of perils faced and conquered in the name of 'Wolves' – free spirits ranging over vast distances in enchanted lands. Maybe, instinctively, I recognised even then my own loneliness and found something of myself in the image of the solitary wolf – and yet they hunt in packs, too, these elemental creatures, sharing their animal warmth, seeking comfort in the company of one another. Wolves: the stuff of dreams; a name to conjure with. About a crowd called the Baggies you could write a limerick; about Wolves you could create an epic.

'Crap,' William said, when I tried to explain all this to him over a pint in a Birmingham pub.

William is a journalist; we had become friends not long after my arrival in Wolverhampton. He'd sought me out, astonished by what he'd heard about some lunatic who'd moved from the west of Ireland to spend a season following Wolves. William, I should add, is a Baggies supporter, a season-ticket man at The Hawthorns.

'Crap,' he said again. William's eloquence often deserts him when talking about Wolves: in his stunted vocabulary – stunted I must repeat, only in the context of Molineux – I hear the sad echoes of too many afternoons chanting too many mindless insults at The Hawthorns.

Despite his Baggies lineage, William is a civilised fellow. He's a graduate of one of England's most esteemed redbrick universities and, despite his youth, can name two hit singles by Buddy Holly and three by Dusty Springfield. Courteous though he is, however, William explained to me that it would not be a good idea for us to go together to the Wolves–Baggies game at The Hawthorns. He needed, he said, to be among his own kind at that game. No offence, mate.

I sensed what William meant as soon as I set foot in The Hawthorns on that last Sunday in November. The hostility here was palpable, like something Saddam Hussein might have developed for chemical warfare against anyone who failed to adore him. John Hendley, a regular contributor to Molineux match programmes, was seated next to me but we were surrounded by Albion supporters. Conscious, perhaps, of my arm-pumping excitability on match days, John leaned towards me and offered the following half-whispered advice: that even if Robbie Keane scored a magical 30-yard goal with a left-footed flick over his shoulder, I'd be well advised to keep my mouth shut, my arms at my side and my rear-end on its seat. No offence, mate.

I heeded John's advice. I also heeded the Albion singing even before the kick-off: 'Fuck off, Wanderers', they sang with gusto all round the ground.

But the omens were good. Robbie would be on from the kick-off, his first start in ten games. We had Birmingham's local scalp freshly under our belt and, just the day before, the Molineux board had confirmed Colin Lee as Wolves' manager – until the end of the season. Colin's caretaker record of three victories and a draw deserved nothing less. All in all, therefore, we had good reason to be optimistic. The Baggies were even more inconsistent than ourselves and gratifyingly, were six places and five points below us in the league table . . . not to mention that their ground is a tawdry place, compared with the splendour of the golden palace at Molineux.

Ours were the better opportunities in a frantic first half. After 15 minutes Robbie had a half-chance but his weak shot along the ground went straight into Miller's arms. Two minutes later a Wolves free kick led to a scramble in the Albion penalty area which ended with Connolly's header over the bar. In the 20th minute Miller saved a strong, left-foot volley from Osborn. Near the half-hour mark, Robbie jinked his way past three opponents but then ran out of space and support. With nine minutes to go to half-time, Lee Hughes, top scorer in the league, went down in our penalty area and the crowd bayed for a penalty. Referee Mr D. Laws said no and was promptly dubbed a wanker by the massed Hawthorns choir. When Mr Laws did blow for half-time, it was still scoreless and I was confident. But quietly so, with my mouth shut and my arms folded.

The ref. had barely whistled for the resumption when everything went wrong. Mario Bortolazzi gently tapped a free kick towards Kevin Kilbane – but there was nothing gentle about Kilbane's strike: his full-blooded shot, from 25 yards, was unstoppable.

One–nil to Albion. The Hawthorns were ecstatic. In the tumult nobody noticed that my mouth was still shut and my arms were unraised in triumph.

Fifteen minutes later we were 2–0 down. Stowell failed to collect a Bortolazzi corner, Richards and Curle were marked absent, and Murphy nudged the ball into our net. Cheers turned to jeers when, a few minutes later, Robbie went off, to be replaced by Niestroj. The game was beyond our reach then, and we knew it. The Albion knew it too: they put away their chanted obscenities and began to sing Psalm 23: 'The Lord Is My Shepherd'.

I had been told, before my visit, of this eccentric Albion custom but, even so, I was fascinated by it. How could these mouths, out of which only venom-laden obscenities had been hurled up to now, suddenly produce these gentle, prayerful words?

It was a relief to head home to Wolverhampton along the M6 in the darkening Sunday afternoon. My first visit to the Hawthorns had left me feeling queasy, as though I had stumbled into some unpleasant half-darkness. I could understand now why so many of the Molineux faithful never ventured into Baggyland.

16

Emblen's Fire

Our fixture list from mid-November to the end of December represented the most demanding phase of the 1998–99 campaign. Steve Bull was still missing — many of us felt he might never again play for Wolves — but even with a fit Bully to lead the attack, the following programme would have been daunting:

Nov 14 – - - — — - - – Norwich (A)
Nov 22 – - - — - - - - – Birmingham (H)
Nov 29 – - - - - - - - – West Brom (A)
Dec 5 – - - - - - - - – Bolton (H)
Dec 12 – - - - - - - - – Norwich (H)
Dec 19 – - - - - - - - – Bradford (A)
Dec 26 – - - - - - - - – Swindon (A)
Dec 28 – - - - - - - - – Ipswich (H)

Only Swindon might be eliminated from this list as play-off contenders; the rest were serious opponents. The last three games in November yielded a break-even points haul but, facing a five-match December, we knew that such a strike rate would not be enough to take us into the top six. Above all, we knew that our attack lacked height and physical strength: we needed a partner up front for Robbie, someone to take the heat off his slight frame, to carve space for him, to knock the ball down for him. With such a partner, we knew the potential: playing alongside the lanky Niall Quinn, Robbie had scored twice for the Republic of Ireland against Croatia who, in the summer of 1998, had finished third in the World Cup in France. There were rumours of a new signing but we began that testing December campaign with more hope than confidence.

Our game against Bolton was played at Molineux on a bitterly cold afternoon. Early on in the match Carl Robinson had the ball in the Bolton net but Robbie Keane was adjudged to have been offside and the score was disallowed. It was still 0–0 at half-time. Around me, as I sipped at my polystyrene cup of warming soup, I could hear the discontent about Robinson's disallowed effort – Robbie, according to our prejudiced consensus, had not been interfering with the play.

Fourteen minutes into the second half we were a goal down. Stowell left his line but failed to gather a deep, diagonal cross and Bob Taylor put Bolton ahead.

That goal brought the best out of the Molineux crowd. As if prompted by a communal cue, the ground roared on its local heroes. Once more we were chasing the game but at least the eleven men on the pitch knew they were not alone.

Neil Emblen turned the game. The roar of welcome, when he replaced Steve Corica in the 20th minute of the second half, left you in no doubt about what the fans thought of Neil Emblen. Emblen is a great-hearted player whose surging runs up the field can bring Molineux to its feet; he's the kind of player who seems to think that stone walls are there to be run through. He was hardly on the pitch when one of those powerful runs of his forced a corner; in the scramble that followed, you wondered how the ball stayed out of the Bolton net. The crowd bayed; Wolves piled on the pressure. Another corner followed and, after a bout of head-tennis, Emblen bundled both ball and Bolton keeper over the line. You had the feeling that, if the Bolton team coach had been in his way, Neil would have headed that into the net as well.

It was by no means a one-man show, but Emblen was undoubtedly the man of the match. In the last minute of the match, as Wolves pressed relentlessly for the winner, it was Neil who again forced one last corner and it was his flying header which went barely wide in the dying seconds.

It finished a 1–1 draw but it had been a courageous effort, a display to warm the cockles of your heart on a bitter day.

After the game I listened to Colin Todd, the Bolton manager, opine that Neil Emblen's goal might have been disallowed had it come from the away side, but he said it without rancour: he'd been long enough in the game, as player and manager, to know that you cannot legislate for such bounces of the ball. And besides, as he well knew, his side had been fortunate not to be a goal behind just a few minutes after the kick-off.

We had salvaged a point, we told ourselves; we tried to forget that we had dropped another two points from a home game. It was not the stuff of which promotion dreams are made.

Next day, on television, I watched as the draw was made for the Third Round of the FA Cup. We were drawn away – to Bolton Wanderers.

17

A Champagne Recovery

The champagne tasted good; so did the poached salmon lunch. The white, linen tablecloth was matched by an array of crisp napkins, creased and folded like Andalusian fans. Under the restaurant lights, silver cutlery shone and crystal glassware sparkled. Through the wide windows we had a panoramic view of the ground – on the pitch, the players were warming up; in the stands, the fans were slowly taking their seats.

You could get used to this kind of match-day schedule, I thought – all this comfort and cosseting, all this good food and drink brought to your table by attentive staff who were always friendly but never presumptuous.

This was the President's Club at Molineux, where more than the food and service were first class; so was the company. For the visit of Norwich, I was the guest of Gerry Zacaroli, a long-time member of this club for fans whose enthusiasm for Wolves is matched by the resilience of their credit cards. Our company around the table included an ebullient Maltese businessman and a softly spoken Shropshire farmer, David Maddocks, together with his two sons and a daughter-in-law. The President's Club is executive-level Wolves fans at play: it has its own sense of style but it shares the same memories and the same hopes as the pie-and-soup folks beyond the plate-glass windows.

Irish interloper though I was, I was welcomed to this fold as if they had long been expecting me. Among these people, my lunacy required no explanation. You were Wolves because who else could you possibly want to be?

I'd been contacted by Gerry Zacaroli following an interview I'd done with Jenny Wilkes on BBC Radio West Midlands shortly after my arrival in Wolverhampton. Jenny, herself a dyed-in-the-polyester Wolves fan, had interviewed me at some length on her afternoon WM show about my personal insanity, my journey from Galway to Molineux and the book I was writing about the current season. It was my good fortune that Gerry happened to hear that interview; recognising in my story a kindred daftness, he called the station and began a friendship. There's good stuff in this fellow: five or six years ago he contracted cancer but, with humour and courage, he conquered both the disease and the treatment and lived to tell the tale.

One of his most treasured memories is of the day when, disconsolate on his hospital bed, he opened his eyes to find Steve Bull at his bedside . . . Bully had a gift too, apart from his welcome presence: a large-format, hardback book entitled *WOLVES: The Complete Record* by Tony Matthews with Les Smith. For much of that season, while I was writing this work, that book rested on my table in Tettenhall Road: I turned to its reference pages, yes, but sometimes I just opened it at the flyleaf, to look at the inscription: '*To Gerry, All the Best, Steve Bull*'. I'd look at the blocked words and the sprawling signature and I'd see in my mind's eye two men who shared a loyalty, the one leaping out of his skin with an athlete's fitness, the other unsure if he would survive, and in that mental image I found my own certainty: that, truly and deeply, this club is about the bond of shared dreams as much as it is about football.

Sometimes, too, absurdity comes sidling in the door. Like all the other men in the President's Club that day, I was wearing a tie. The club enforces a strict dress code: tie-less males are not admitted, not even Sir Jack himself, according to the stories. Jeans are strictly forbidden, regardless of whether they are covering male or female bottoms. A couple of weeks before the Norwich game, one corporate guest had presented himself, properly clad in jacket and tie, at one of the hospitality suites, but had been refused admission on the grounds that he was wearing jeans. The Molineux steward was unmoved by protests: jeans were forbidden by the club regulations and that was that. Our corporate guest was miffed but he was also resourceful: he took himself off at once to buy some new George gear at the Asda supermarket across the road from Molineux. Minutes later the club steward was astonished to find himself confronted by a strapping, six-foot male wearing a jacket and tie over a tiny microskirt that displayed a pair of hairy legs to full advantage. The rules, apparently, made no reference to men in minis: game, set and match to our guest.

It seemed strange to be playing Norwich again, so soon after the trip to Carrow Road: the closeness of the two fixtures, I figured, was down to a computer kink. There was a further oddity about the sequence of games: this was our 23rd match, the final game in the first half of the 46-match season. Playing Norwich twice in the first half was balanced by not having met Bradford at all as yet.

Norwich themselves seemed strange. In their away strip of black with luminous green-and-off-yellow vertical stripes, these Canaries looked like the mutant produce of some post-nuclear holocaust. The crowd was small for Molineux, just over 21,000. Maybe the cold, bitter day was keeping them away; maybe it was the financial demands of Christmas. It was too soon, I hoped, for the fans to have decided that our promotion prospects also belonged in some distant, distorted future.

Wolves' bright beginning gave no indication of the shape the game would take. A few minutes after the kick-off, Robbie was presented with a through ball but he hesitated, as if thinking he were offside, and the chance was gone. In the eighth minute Lee Naylor, persevering on the left, put in a good cross and Robbie's left-foot volley was saved only by a brilliant effort from Watt in the Norwich goal. A few minutes later a daft challenge on Russell earned Sedgley a yellow card; the crowd immediately dubbed referee Kirkby a wanker. (Onanism seems a congenital attribute of referees.) In our presidential club seats we laughed at the chanting but we refrained from joining in.

But halfway through the first half we shared in the anger which erupted around the stadium. Carl Robinson's shot, following a brilliant passing movement, was well saved by the Norwich goalie but the ball was then palmed away by a Norwich defender. At the time I couldn't spot which defender — I learned later it was Adams — but, like the rest of the stadium, I clearly saw the ball being knocked away off the line by a Norwich hand. Without doubt, it should have been a penalty.

A penalty was awarded ten minutes later — but it was given the other way, for a foul by Dean Richards on Iwan Roberts. Adams scored. This was Bolton re-visited. Against the run of play, we were a goal down.

The referee and his assistants inevitably became the focus of the crowd's frustration. The Norwich contingent, strangely silent up to now, suddenly found their voice and began to massage our anger. 'If this was South America,' they chanted, 'they'd never leave the pitch.'

When the teams did leave the pitch for half-time, it was still 1–0 to Norwich. Twenty minutes after the re-start, our visitors were two goals in front: ex-Wolves man, Iwan Roberts, headed in from the far post and the game seemed beyond our reach.

Colin Lee's response was to replace Sedgley and Whittingham with Michael Gilkes and David Connolly.

Kevin Muscat's response was a ferocious 50:50 challenge for the ball, just outside the box, on Craig Bellamy. The Australian rarely comes second-best out of these confrontations: the young Norwich player crumpled on the pitch while on the sideline his manager, Bruce Rioch, erupted in fury. For a few seconds, chaos threatened to tip over into ugliness. Rioch was restrained by his own colleagues and the unfortunate Bellamy was stretchered off to have his knee stitched. Muscat escaped without a card of either colour.

Only ten minutes remained, and we were still two goals behind, when Simon Osborn was replaced by Neil Emblen. The roar that greeted Emblen's appearance seemed to galvanise the entire team. Neil was some three minutes on the pitch when he managed to get on the end of a Michael Gilkes cross but his header was saved by Watt; Robbie, however, was at hand and his left-foot shot was low and true. Seven minutes left and still a goal down. Only a minute remained when Robbie found the net again, this time with a headed ball from another Gilkes cross.

Molineux erupted – including the dignified confines of the President's Club. It was the most spectacular fight-back I had seen, the most joyful day I had so far experienced at Molineux. After the Carrow Road game, when a ten-man Norwich had hung on for a draw, Bruce Rioch had opined that Colin Lee would be less pleased than himself with a drawn point; I felt sure he'd feel differently now, after giving up a two-goal lead.

We had shown that we possessed character, useful substitutes and the will to fight back. The net result of our spectacular fight-back, however, at this halfway stage of the campaign, was that we were clinging by our bootlaces to the top half of the table: we were in 12th place in our division of 24 teams. At the press conference after the game someone pointed out to Colin Lee how admirable and reassuring it was that Wolves could come back from behind to salvage a win or a draw; ah yes,

Colin said with a shrug and a smile, but it would be so much more comfortable if we could just get in front from the beginning. And so say all of us.

18
Lost in Bradford

I got lost in Bradford. A wrong exit off the big roundabout at the end of the M606 left me driving downhill on a wide carriageway that runs like a wound across the city. Under a low December sky the city was grey and dismal. As I edged along in the slow lane, vainly searching for a sign for the Valley Parade, I recalled how, years earlier, the appointment of a tourist officer for this city had been the subject of eyebrow-arched comment in the press. I understood the raised eyebrows now. You might holiday here after you'd been to bombed-out Beirut and siege-struck Sarajevo.

Or you might come here to meet the people. They were friendly. The fellow with the leather jacket and the claret-and-amber scarf couldn't be more helpful: he'd be glad to take me to the ground himself but he had to meet his mates for a few pints before the game. He stooped towards my open window and gave precise, finger-pointing directions that I still recall with clarity: up the hill, right at Morrisons, left, right again, then left at the roundabout and you can't miss it.

And I couldn't. I drove up on the footpath, angled alongside the other cars that, even at one o'clock, were already crowding the area at the back of the ground. They were friendly, too, in the caff I found up on the busy road at the other side of the stadium. Pictures of the Italian national side jostled on the walls with shots of the local side; the youngster who handed me the huge mug of instant coffee looked distinctly Mediterranean. The fellow on the stool at the tiny counter looked distinctly local: shorn haircut, jeans, checked shirt with the sleeves rolled up to show off powerful forearms that were tattooed in dark, snaky patterns from wrist to elbow. Yet somehow he was unmenacing: maybe it was the soft Yorkshire burr, maybe it was the comforting clack of pool balls from the area behind us – whatever it was, we had the kind of chat that is at the heart of football: points won and lost, hopes spoken and then shrugged away, as though too much optimism might be bad for you. Bradford were in a stronger position than we were: in fifth place after a shaky start in which they had won only once in their opening five games. Our own first five games – four wins and a draw – had almost become less than a memory. I lingered a while with my tattooed acquaintance; I was in no hurry to exchange the steamed-up warmth of the café for the bitter cold of the afternoon.

It got colder. Sitting among the Bradford fans in a corner of the new stand, I thought that all my extremities must surely fall off. My neighbours didn't seem to mind. Maybe they're just used to northern winters. Or maybe they were warmed by events on the pitch. After 20 minutes Robbie Blake put the Bantams ahead, side-stepping Dean Richards, a former Bradford player, before left-footing the ball into the net. Six minutes after half-time, Bradford were two goals ahead: Stowell had made yet another brilliant save but, after a scramble in the box, Lee Mills' left-foot drive into the roof of the net gave our keeper no chance. Mills was an irony we could only regret. A former Wolves player, he had matured into a powerful striker and was Bradford's top goal-scorer. Big and strong, he was just the kind of partner many of us wished to see playing alongside the slighter figure of Robbie Keane.

Robbie got one back for us, midway through the second half, but you'd have to admit it was against the run of play. Only the brilliance of Mike Stowell kept the score at 2–1: for me, Stowell was the man of the match. He played like a man inspired, parrying blasters from all sides with a kind of manic elation. At least Mike's fingers would be warm; as the end neared, mine seemed frozen to the pen, scribbling my notes on my pad. Smoke swirled around me: the smokers, I reasoned, were not offering dubious homage to the memory of the fans who had died in the Valley Parade fire – they were just striking matches to warm themselves.

The Bradford Valley game was our last match before Christmas. The win lifted Bradford into third place, behind second-placed Ipswich and Sunderland, who looked as if they were going to run away with the championship. The Sunday newspapers, I guessed, would have a field-day with manager Paul Jewell's success – clichés about gems and crowns and diamonds would inevitably litter the columns of the back pages (at least in those newspapers which recognised the existence of footballing life outside the Premiership). I, too, would be happy enough if Santa brought a couple of clichéd gifts to Molineux for Christmas – up front, a big striker with aerial power and, at the back, the gift of a watertight defence.

19

Christmas Day

I had decided to remain in Wolverhampton for Christmas. Most times, I'm easy with my own company; there didn't seem to be too much difference between being solitary in my house in Galway and being alone in the flat on Tettenhall Road. Besides, the week after Christmas Day held lengthy football trips to the south-west and the north-west.

On Christmas morning I went to church; the liturgy was both uninspired and uninspiring, so I shall leave the church unnamed. Throughout the day the phone rang – first my son, then my daughters; later in the evening I had calls from a brother and one of my sisters. I prepared my Christmas feast: £2.99 for roast turkey, stuffing, roast potatoes and chipolata sausages, all from the Marks & Sparks kitchen – what more could a solitary writer ask for?

My children, on the phone, all wanted to know what I was doing with myself for the big day; the notion of spending it alone was alien to them, as they always spend the day with their mother. Inevitably, as the day wore on and the relentless rain continued to pound on the car-park outside my flat, I found myself visiting Christmases past, when my children were little and we had all lived together in a lovely, old house on Dublin's Park Avenue. The old cliché is true: Christmas means little without children, the breathless expectancy of Christmas Eve bedtime and the mesmerising excitement of the morning when you are roused at an ungodly hour to have the harvest of the night brandished triumphantly in your protesting eyes and ears. You blink and all those Christmas mornings are suddenly gone: your son and your daughters are young adults and you are on your own in a flat in Wolverhampton.

20

An End-of-Year Bonus

Boxing Day 1998 was the kind of day you'd prefer to forget. Then again, in another way, it was the sort of day that every travelling football fan worth his strip simply has to endure at least once a season: a rite of passage, a winning of studs.

The day trip to Swindon had all the ingredients of a nightmare: abominable weather conditions, an atrocious pitch and a certifiably unjust result.

And I wasn't even putting up with the worst of it. Although half-numb with the cold, at least I was dry, up in the last row of the Arkell Stand. I could only pity my fellow Wolves fans, huddled together in the unroofed pen behind the goal on my left. In their white plastic capes they looked like a heap of sodden newspapers that somebody had forgotten to take out of the weather. The capes came courtesy of Nationwide: they were about as useful against the pelting rain as Factor 20 might be against one of Bill Clinton's Scud missiles (or even one of his Cuban cigars). There had been anger back in October when visiting West Brom supporters had been housed there in even worse conditions; from the County Ground had come the promise that our supporters would be allocated the covered stand behind the goal at the other end, but obviously something had gone wrong. Or maybe the powers-that-be at Swindon just figured that what was bad enough for Baggies fans was good enough for Molineux folk.

I shivered, just watching them in their roofless enclosure. Half an hour before the kick-off I left the stand, in search of tea. Or coffee. Or soup. Anything, so long as it was hot.

I found the tea urn, together with a warming smile from the lady in charge of it. With a heart like hers, she was obviously not in charge of the accommodation arrangements for visiting fans.

I also found Fernando Gomez, disconsolate in his Wolves tracksuit, leaning against the door jamb of the press room, apparently watching the TV on the opposite wall. Fernando and I had spoken a couple of times – once at the training ground, once up at Huddersfield. I sympathised with him on his omission from the line-up but the Spaniard was grim. He wanted to play, he said, but apparently he didn't fit in with the manager's plans. You never know, I said, injuries and illnesses could have you back in for the next game. Prophetic words, although I didn't know it then. As we stood talking in the doorway, I wanted only to cheer Fernando up: I liked his attitude, the way he said it wasn't enough to draw his wages – he wanted to wear our black-and-gold shirt. Besides, I admired his intelligent style of play and I told him so. We swapped phone numbers and New Year greetings and parted – Fernando to the dressing-room, myself to my seat in the Arkell.

The pitch was a casserole; you wondered why this game had not been numbered among the many postponements inflicted by the Boxing Day weather. Probably all for the best – get it over with, collect the three points and then survive the motorway journey back up to the Black Country. I felt that only the weather could beat us here – a bad bounce, a back-pass trapped in the mud, something daft you couldn't legislate for. We'd beaten Swindon 1–0 up at Molineux in the balmy days of August; manager Steve McMahon had given up the ghost since then, unable any longer to submit himself and his family to the abuse of hostile supporters. Jimmy Quinn had taken over as manager but Swindon, although they had beaten Barnsley 3–1 away the previous week, just didn't seem like fearsome opposition.

That too was how the game began to unfold on the soggy pitch. Mark Atkins's left-foot curler was just wide after three minutes. On the quarter-hour Robbie tried to lob Talia, the Swindon keeper, but the wind gusted his lightly weighted effort wide. Six minutes later his goal-bound shot was headed off the Swindon line by a last-gasp defender.

As the first half wore on, Swindon came more into the game. Sustained pressure coming up to the half-hour brought them four consecutive corners; only Stowell's brilliant tip-over save kept them out. The Swindon fans bayed; ours shivered in the wind and rain.

The rain suddenly stopped, with eleven minutes to go to half-time. It was the signal for Keith Curle to floor Robin Hulbert on the half-way line; our captain was fortunate not to receive his marching orders. The resulting free kick created panic in our defence but somehow the ball was scrambled clear and I could breathe again. With a minute to go to the interval, Robbie seemed through but he was forced wide and the ball went out for a corner. Robbie went down in the box after that but his hopeful glance at the referee drew only jeers from the Swindon crowd. It was still scoreless at half-time and I was no longer so confident of the outcome.

Five minutes after the re-start, Neil Emblen, pushing forward in his first start since our win over Sheffield United, forced the concession of a corner. In the next two minutes we won three more corners in rapid succession but failed to put the ball into the net. Our Irish strike-force of Robbie Keane and David Connolly just wasn't clicking: there were rumours that these two didn't see eye-to-eye off the pitch. The rain started again, gusting in great drenching squalls towards our supporters' end. So did the hand-clapping, foot-stomping, Swindon chanting: 'JIMMY QUINN'S BARMY ARMY.' There was a relentless mindlessness about it that made you wonder about the local supporters.

The match seemed destined to end scoreless. We were clearly on top in the closing minutes but the red defence was somehow holding us at bay and it looked as if we'd be heading back up the M42 with only a single point in the bag.

Then, in the dying seconds, Steve Sedgley gave away an unnecessary free kick on the edge of the box. Mark Walters, who had replaced Hulbert in the second half, drove the free kick high into the box; Keith Curle and Dean Richards stood as if rooted in the Swindon mud and Onuora rose for a free header that was straight and true. There was barely time to kick-off before referee Stretton blew time.

Once again, a game that we had dominated had been snatched from us in the final seconds. Or maybe we just gave it away.

It was, up to that point, the most sickening day of my season-long campaign with Wolves. I could only hope that I would not have to suffer another one like it.

Our unsheltered fans had suffered even more. I thought about them, as I sat in the small Rover alongside David Instone of the *Express and Star*, heading up the motorway in the rain and the dark. How must they feel, drenched to the bone, making their long and pointless journey home?

Throughout the long, soaked afternoon they had cheered and chanted; they had stayed, drenched and frozen, to the sad and bitter end. They deserved better.

★

Two days later they got it. On Monday, 28 December, we had a one o'clock kick-off at Molineux against Ipswich.

The Christmas-break attendance, in excess of 24,000, was the largest since the September game against Sunderland, but the omens looked unpromising. Ipswich were lying second in the table, only five points behind Sunderland; furthermore, their 2–0 win over us at Portman Road had been more comprehensive than the scoreline would suggest. That result had been the straw that broke Mark McGhee's managerial back at Molineux and led to the appointment of Colin Lee as manager, but there were other changes in the Wolves format which were less welcome on that chilly afternoon.

David Connolly was out with tendonitis; more crucially, Robbie Keane was sidelined with flu. This gave a debut start to our German import, Robert Niestroj. Fernando was on the bench, his first time in a match squad since the game at Sheffield on 10 November. Neil Emblen, utility man *par excellence*, was paired up front with Guy Whittingham – the game was the last of Whitty's loan period at Molineux.

Early on, we took the game to Ipswich, with Niestroj, in particular, battling hard and effectively in midfield, but still the longed-for goal eluded us. The game seemed becalmed for the second period of that first half, as though the players were too sated with Christmas fare to show much interest in exerting themselves.

At half-time, frustrated by our inability to get the goal we deserved, I was pontificating over a polystyrene cup of soup to Geoff Owen and Ron Warillow. Geoff records the Wolves Clubcall service; Ron has been reporting on Wolves and Albion games since he got out of short trousers.

'We should bring on Fernando,' I said. 'We need someone in the middle to carve out a few chances for us up front.'

My companions were amused by my essay into management.

'All right, then,' Geoff said, 'you're the manager – who're you taking off to bring Fernando on?'

I had to think about that one.

'Osborn,' I said at last. 'We'll take Osborn off and bring on Fernando.'

The press room at Molineux was obviously bugged. Halfway through the second half, Colin Lee replaced Simon Osborn with Fernando and the Spaniard made an almost immediate impact, giving us control of the midfield. For all our efforts, the winner still looked beyond us.

When it came, it was all the sweeter for its lateness. Fernando touched on a throw-in from the left side and Kevin Muscat, running on to it, struck the sweetest goal you could hope to see in a month of Saturdays. It was a rising, swerving shot which left the Ipswich goalkeeper moving to his right before it rocketed high into the other side of the net.

Molineux went wild. Christmas had seemed to have bypassed us but now, belatedly, Santa Claus had remembered us . . . and it was flattering to realise that Colin Lee had been eavesdropping on my interval discussions in the Molineux press room.

Apart from our haul of three precious points, the result was significant in other ways. It was only the second time in the season that Ipswich had been beaten away from home and it was Wolves' first victory since Colin Lee had been given the job of full-time manager.

That eight-game sequence of difficult games, beginning away to Norwich and ending here at home to Ipswich, had yielded only two wins and three draws: a harvest of nine points out of a possible total of 24 was hardly the stuff of promotion potential.

In the post-match euphoria of 28 December, there was no room for such negative realism. We had, at last, got the rub of the green and the last game of 1998 had given us a memory to treasure.

21

New Year's Eve 1998

New Year's Eve was a grey and bitterly cold day in Wolverhampton. I spent an hour or so that morning watching John Ward put the team through their defensive paces on the Newbridge training ground. John had been a casualty of a managerial shake-up at Bristol but, on the ever-spinning football carousel, he had quickly found a slot as number two to the newly installed Colin Lee at Molineux. It was, in many ways, a fortuitous move for John as he had maintained his family home in the Midlands throughout his time at Bristol. Watching him at work on that chilly December morning, I felt it had been a good move for Wolves as well.

John worked the players in pairs at first, one-on-one, in a confined space no bigger than the service box of a tennis court. The emphasis was on defence: the defender had to stay tight, shadowing and harrying his opponent but without making the irretrievable – and ineffective – tackle which would allow the attacker through to score. I noticed how he shouted encouragement not only at the defenders but also at the probing attackers. The practice area was widened then, to allow two-on-two, but each pair had to remain inside their own tramlines: the aim was controlled defence and staying on your feet. There was more of the same after that, with four facing four, on the full width of a pitch. The players' panted breaths hung like smoke in the frosty air; their grunts and shouts were loud in the empty space.

I was joined on my sloping vantage point by a thirty-something daddy with his youngster at heel. Father and son wore Wolves jackets and woollen caps; they'd travelled 40 miles for this first trip to see their heroes on the training pitch. It was a New Year's treat for them both; the boy was cradling in his arms a new full-size football. As the training session ended and the players began to leave the pitch in animated groups, my two companions chased after them with shouted goodbyes. Watching Robbie and the rest of them signing their names with the fat felt-tip on the boy's new football made me realise all over again why I had come to Wolverhampton: there was magic here. The boy knew it, so did his father. The magic was sparkling, there on that frosty pitch, as the players cheerfully and patiently autographed the youngster's football. I doubt, somehow, that that ball will ever be kicked on a playing pitch: years hence, a grown man will treasure it, turning it with wonder in his hands, remembering a long-ago New Year's Eve when his dad took him to Newbridge and the gods stooped down to speak to him.

I caught up with Colin Lee halfway across the pitch and introduced myself to him, explaining why I was there and about my Galway background. Colin listened with the same attentiveness and spoke with the same courtesy that I had noticed in him at post-match press conferences. Yes, he agreed, morale was high in the squad that morning, despite the flu and injuries that had laid low so many of the players; sometimes, he went on, it was just such misfortunes that brought out the best in the remainder of the squad. The presence of Robbie Keane on the pitch that morning was a completely unexpected bonus; he hadn't been expected to recover from a heavy flu for another few days – but, said Colin, it was the kind of willingness that was typical of Robbie.

The squad would train again on the afternoon of New Year's Day, Colin said, in answer to my question, before heading up the motorway by coach for Saturday's cup clash with Bolton. We said goodbye when we reached Colin's car in the parking area. Afterwards I sat a while in my own car, marvelling at the gifts the New Year had brought me: I had walked off the training ground with the Wolves manager and had been spoken to with interest and friendliness.

It was hard to believe that only six months previously I had been sitting at my kitchen table in Galway, in my house high up on the hill that overlooked the sleepy bay. I had grown tired of the beautiful view; I had tired, too, of the novel I was working on, even though I was well into it and could see where it was taking itself. Solitude is essential to the writer's work but, early in that summer of 1998, it weighed heavily upon me.

For many years I had harboured the notion of writing a book about a season on the trail of Wolves, but I had kept my notions to myself: the idea of swapping my home in Galway for a football base in Wolverhampton seemed too preposterous ever to be spoken aloud. Yet, when I took my courage in my hands and hesitantly voiced my crazy notion on the phone, first to my agent in London and then to Bill Campbell at Mainstream Publishing in Edinburgh, neither of them seemed to think the idea was totally outrageous. Within a few days, contracts were exchanged and I was loading a few bits and pieces into my old Kadett for the long haul to Wolverhampton. I was excited, but I was frightened too by the suddenness of it all; an old proverb that I had learned from a classics professor at college surfaced from my memory: 'Beware lest your dreams come true.'

Less than six months had passed since that journey; in that brief span I had fallen into a new and different way of life. When I was stopped in the lower reaches of Dudley Street on the afternoon of New Year's Eve and asked by a passer-by for directions to Lichfield Street, I felt oddly triumphant in being able to help: I was no longer a complete stranger on these Black Country streets.

That same afternoon, I had a cuppa in Drucker's with Ray, one of my regular away-day travelling companions. Inevitably, we mulled over Wolves' progress and our hopes of promotion. I was more optimistic than Ray, perhaps because of the bubbling camaraderie I had witnessed that morning on the training ground; Ray, in any case, had suffered more false Wolves dawns than he wished to remember. To make the play-offs – automatic promotion from first or second place now seemed a truly impossible dream – we would need a sustained run of good results early in the new year.

On New Year's Eve 1998, the top half of Division One looked like this:

Place	Team	P	W	D	L	Pts
1.	Sunderland	26	16	8	2	56
2.	Ipswich	26	14	6	6	48
3.	Birmingham	26	13	6	7	45
4.	Bradford	25	13	5	7	44
5.	Bolton	25	11	10	4	43
6.	Watford	25	12	7	6	43
7.	Huddersfield	26	12	5	9	41
8.	Grimsby	26	12	5	8	41
9.	Norwich	24	11	7	6	40
10.	West Brom	26	11	5	10	38
11.	Sheffield	26	10	7	9	37
12.	Wolves	26	10	7	9	37

The gap between ourselves and sixth-placed Watford was six points but we had 20 games left to bridge that gap. It was difficult but it was by no means impossible. We needed to tighten up at the back and we needed more penetration up front – the simple universal formula for football success! Steve Bull was still out and the rumours were rife that his knee was so badly injured that he would never play again. Santa Claus, however, had not entirely neglected Molineux: two days before Christmas the news had broken that Wolves were in the process of signing the Norwegian international, Haavard Flo, a tall, lanky attacker who'd played with Werder Bremen in the German *Bundesliga*. He could never replace Bully – nobody could – but this big fellow might be just the ticket to accompany Robbie up front and to get our promotion challenge back into gear once more.

In Drucker's, on that afternoon of New Year's Eve, Ray and myself wished each other luck. It was a commodity rarely seen in recent times at Molineux.

22

The Cup that Cheers

2 January 1999, FA Cup Third Round: Away to Bolton Wanderers
'Last Drop Village', says the signpost at Junction 6 on the M61, and you fear you're headed for some Lancashire equivalent of the Nevada desert. You're not. You lift your eyes and you can see the Reebok Stadium in the near distance. This is a seriously beautiful stadium; its white, curving lines soar gracefully against a backdrop of gently rounded hills. You can see the Premiership money and ambitions in the rich comfort of the ground and in the formal dress and style of stewards and staff. You could sense the frustration, too, with the club's Division One status: Bolton had run away with the same division in 1997 but had been relegated after just one season, unable to compete at Premiership level.

As with Wolves, Bolton's 'today' is overshadowed by all its yesterdays. Along with Wolves, they were one of the 12 founding members of the Football League in 1888. They never managed to capture the First Division title but they were winners of the cup four times. Their most recent cup triumph was in 1958, just two years before Wolves last won the trophy. It was all history but the fabulous new stadium gave notice of the club's aspirations for the twenty-first century.

It also serves as stark evidence of the continuing commercial drift of English football. The Reebok Stadium stands a few miles from the town of Bolton on a greenfield site easily accessible from a network of motorways; on the same site you will find parking for thousands of cars, together with a Warner Village cinema complex, a huge Asda store, and nearly all the fast-food franchises and high street retail outlets that you could mention. It's the flavour of the end of the century: football is a retail activity.

Nat Lofthouse, the greatest of all Bolton players, won his 33 England caps in the era of the 'maximum wage'; back then he could never have even dreamed of the astronomical amounts of money paid to today's footballers. Maybe, in the long run, his reward is greater: Nat Lofthouse is remembered in the name of one of the Reebok's stands and, more importantly, in the hearts of all Bolton football folk.

Colin Lee would have given a pretty penny to be able to include someone like Lofthouse in our line-up that day. Sickness and injuries meant that Robbie Keane would play alone up front with a five-man midfield behind him: Niestroj, Robinson, Fernando, Corica and Gilkes. The back four was made up of Atkins, Emblen, Curle and Muscat. To make up the five substitutes allowed for FA Cup ties, Lee had had to draft in youth team members, Gordon Simms and Adam Proudlock, alongside Lee Naylor, reserve keeper Matt Murray and Glenn Crowe, who had not managed to make even the bench so far that season.

Yet, as Fernando kicked off, I was optimistic: the commitment and high spirits that I had sensed on the training ground led me to believe that, depleted as we were, we were still in with a good shout.

We certainly dictated the opening exchanges – off the pitch. To my right, Wolves supporters had released a whole sea of black-and-gold balloons which ebbed and flowed behind Bolton's goal. As the black-and-gold rubber waves threatened to engulf Jussi Jaaskelainen, the Icelandic keeper, referee Mr D'Urso stopped the game while stewards took remedial action. For some minutes, much to the mirth of the Wolfpack, the air was loud with the sounds of balloon-popping, as local stewards stomped on the hapless balloons.

Minutes after the restart, our mirth became exultation. Fernando's through ball reached Robbie, who seemed almost astonished to find himself so alone in so much space but nevertheless rounded the advancing keeper before slotting home with his right boot. After eight minutes we were a goal up. The Wolfpack went crazy; the Lancashire skies were loud with chanted praise of 'KEENO! KEENO!'

The skies must have ached that afternoon, battered by the relentless cheers and jeers and moans and groans of a hypnotised crowd. The game developed into a ding-dong contest – although most of the dings seemed to be donged inside our penalty area. Stowell seemed faultless, playing with the same masterful confidence that had saved us from a real hiding up at Bradford. Bolton swept forward in endless white-shirted waves but somehow our goal remained intact when the half-time whistle blew.

The second half began where the first had left off: Bolton forced a corner in the very first minute. The home crowd bayed for a goal; Gilkes booted clear and, for a second anyway, I could breathe again. Keith Curle took off on an unlikely surging run down the left wing and I thought to myself: Keith's not in the mood to give in easily today. Maybe, just maybe, we'll hold out. I checked my watch: only 44 minutes to go . . .

There were moments when we lifted the siege. In the eighth minute of the second half Fernando headed a lovely through ball into Robbie's path but our boy-hero's left-foot measured shot was well saved by the Bolton Icelander.

We finally cracked 13 minutes into the half. From yet another Bolton corner, Scott Sellars took possession and the Reebok exploded as he lashed an unstoppable diagonal shot into the roof of our net. One-all, over half an hour to go and Bolton on the rampage: it looked to be all over for us.

Just two minutes later the locals were on their feet again as Dean Holdsworth rounded Stowell and put the ball in the net with his right foot, only to be whistled back for offside.

And then, five minutes later, as the floodlights grew brighter in the deepening darkness, it was Robbie to the rescue again. On a rare visit upfield Niestroj whipped a shot across the Bolton goal and Robbie was there, diving forward to head us once more into the lead.

The Reebok was stunned but 25 minutes remained, more than enough time for Bolton to impose themselves on the game.

Somehow they couldn't.

Somehow Wolves held out.

Somehow I didn't get a coronary as Bolton launched attack after attack and Wolves defended with desperation. Minutes crawled by. Fifteen to go. Thirteen. Eleven . . . the bombardment never let up; it seemed impossible to keep Bolton out.

With a minute of normal time remaining, Bolton forced a corner and we cleared it. Our fans were frantic now, whistling at the ref. for the blessed, last relief. Robbie was harrying and chasing in the Bolton half – anything to keep the ball away from our end. Bolton surged back, the ball was inside our box, Atkins miskicked and it seemed we had lost it then but Kevin Muscat dived in – legally! – with a saving tackle to lash the ball away from a Bolton boot.

The referee played four minutes of extra time that seemed like four lifetimes. To the end, Bolton attacked: their last hurrah was still another corner and then that relieving whistle blew and some Wolves boot belted the ball towards the deafened heavens and the field was ours.

It was the first FA Cup tie I had ever seen: a memorable match in a fabulous stadium – and a result to warm the cockles of your palpitating heart.

24 January, FA Cup Fourth Round: Home to Arsenal
Three weeks later, on an ITV Sunday, Arsenal's posse of international gunslingers rode into the Black Country. Manninger of Austria. Frenchmen Anelka, Petit and Garde. Bergkamp and Overmars from the Netherlands. Not to mention a few Englishmen, among them the captain of the national side, Tony Adams. Every one of them was dutifully booed by a sell-out Molineux as the team announcements were made.

As League and Cup champions, Arsenal were hot favourites but I shared in the defiant optimism that was voiced by fans in the days leading up to the match. Besides, there was a score to settle: Arsenal had beaten Wolves the year before in the semi-final by the only goal of the game – and that had been the result of an unfortunate, miskicked clearance by goalkeeper Hans Seger. Molineux was buzzing and so were the players – during the week before the game, I'd been fortunate enough to be able to speak to Kevin Muscat, Neil Emblen and Haavard Flo and their excitement and commitment for this big clash had been tangible.

It took only ten minutes for things to start going wrong. We were giving as good as we got when Overmars picked up the ball in his own half; there seemed no danger – the Dutchman was a long way from goal and we had a full complement of defenders in position. Overmars went forward at a lope; our defenders backed off; still there seemed no danger. In a flash there was: Overmars accelerated, our defenders obligingly stood off to give him a better view of the goal and the Dutchman picked his spot for a low shot into the left-hand corner of the net. We were a goal down to a shot that should never have been allowed.

Molineux roared its team back into the game. Two minutes later Emblen was wide with a low shot to the left. On the quarter-hour Gilkes hit the crossbar with a shot/cross that had Manninger beaten. Then Robbie was whistled back for offside after a complex passing movement. Outside the Arsenal box Carl Robinson made a brilliant trapping turn but was scythed down by Emmanuel Petit; from the resulting free kick the ball came back to Carl but the chance was awkward and his shot went over the bar.

Nine minutes before half-time we got it right – or maybe the young Austrian in the Arsenal goal got it wrong. Manninger came to gather Muscat's high cross but Flo was faster and higher and his looping header found the Arsenal net. It was a snapshot of contemporary English football: an Australian cross, an Austrian error, a Norwegian goal.

And Black Country bliss. Molineux went wild. If we kept our heads we could see off these arrogant Wenger millionaires.

At half-time it was 1–1 and anybody's game. Robbie Keane, who was rumoured to be a target of Wenger's millions, was having a relatively quiet game but, on the other hand, the Arsenal internationals were not being allowed to play as well as we knew they could.

Thirteen minutes after the re-start we should have gone ahead. Once more Flo, playing only his second game in the black and gold, had Manninger beaten, with the ball loose, but Flo was unbalanced as he connected with the ball . . . it moved weakly towards the unprotected Arsenal goal-line and then, to everybody's horror, it rebounded off the upright. It was one of those moments that you never forget, a moment that would have swung the game for us. Molineux was singing, rousing the Wolves to mightier efforts, but you felt that that old Celestial Director of Football had turned his back on us, up there behind a velvety Molineux sky.

Less than 20 minutes from time you knew it for sure. Stowell yet again saved brilliantly, turning the ball around his post; the corner was cleared, but only to the edge of the box where the waiting Bergkamp struck a hopeful shot that first bounced off the turf before hitting, first, Flo and then Curle for a fortuitous deflected goal.

It was the goal that won the game.

Unfairly, Colin Lee said afterwards, and I agreed with him: Wolves deserved a draw at least.

The next day I read in the papers that the Arsenal manager was upset

ABOVE: Wolf-cub Robbie Keane, seen here on a fruitless dash for goal at the Reebok, was our top-scorer of the 1998–99 campaign, with 16 goals from all competitions

LEFT: Keith Curle, our captain and – sometimes – successful penalty-taker!

Play-anywhere Neil Emblen, seen here tussling with Arsenal's Upton in the 2–1 FA Cup Fourth Round defeat at Molineux, always inspired both his team-mates and the Wolfpack with his never-say-die attitude

Midfield play-maker Simon Osborn, watched by Dean Richards, threads a shot through the Ipswich defence in the 1–0 December win at Molineux

ABOVE: Kevin Muscat, in action here against Birmingham's Brian Hughes, in our 3–1 victory at Molineux. For skill, courage and indomitable spirit, Muscat was my personal Player of the Year

LEFT: Viking Wolf embraces Aussie Wolf: Haavard Flo celebrates his goal against Crewe with Steve Corica. The game ended 3–0 to Wolves

Long before the end of the season, veteran Spanish international Fernando Gómez could hear the roll of the drums for his exit from Molineux: for me, his elegant, intelligent passing will remain a thing of beauty

Colin Lee and John Ward salute the Wolfpack after a fighting 1–1 draw with Bolton at the Reebok. That Friday night the dream of play-offs and promotion was still alive: but a few nights later, at Grimsby, our banners lay in tatters on the Cleethorpes sand . . .

We wondered, as Colin Lee signalled the introduction of Steve Bull on the final day of the season against Bradford, whether we were watching the last appearance of the Wolves legend in the old-gold and black

Michael Gilkes in action against Birmingham's Peter Ndlovu. When I bumped into Michael at a Wolverhampton watering-hole not long after the season ended, he made no attempt to conceal his distress at not being offered a new contract at Molineux

We shall not look upon his like again. A month after the season's end, Steve Bull finally gave up the unequal struggle with a dodgy knee and announced his retirement

In the last minutes of a dying season, Mike Stowell finds the strength and the agility to tip over a Bradford penalty. The unsmiling faces of the Wolfpack tell the sad truth that even Stowell's brilliance could not save another lost campaign

Molineux cameraman Peter Harrington took this shot of me just a few hours after Bradford had finally buried our dreams in the Black Country sunshine. I can only imagine that I was smiling at the prospect of another season to come, another journey to travel in hope

by the late red card given to Petit for abusing a linesman; also that his Arsenal side were often simply 'too nice'. I never did get to see Monsieur Wenger close up, in the authentic flesh: he had no time to spare for the assembled scribes in the Molineux press room. One hack was admitted to his august presence but, when he returned to the rest of us with 'Arsene's quotes', I figured it was time for me to leave. I was in no humour to listen to some latter-day Moses reading out the new commandments from the eminence of the new Mount Sinai at Highbury.

23

Fame – At Last!

We all knew that our cup adventures, exciting as they were, were still no more than a side-show: the main feature remained, as ever, the push for promotion. As a boy in Galway in the 1950s, the cup had always seemed to me infinitely more important than the league; maybe it always does to a boy. There truly is something magical about the notion of Doncaster Rovers, say, overturning the likes of Manchester United; it has all the fabulous appeal of those tales where the beggar becomes the king and the ordained order of things is stood on its po-faced head. At least to boys – and especially if you don't support Man U. As a boy I loved such 'doughty Cup-fighters'; as a man I wonder why I have never seen that lovely word 'doughty' used in any other context . . .

Tranmere Rovers might be doughty but they showed little doughtiness for our first league game of 1999. I didn't travel for this match, the first of two league games that Wolves played between their Third and Fourth Round FA Cup ties. On that Friday night I was in Dublin – even Wolves had to take a natural back seat for my daughter Georgia's 21st birthday.

The Sky TV cameras were at Preston Park that night, bringing live coverage of the game; when I sneaked away from my daughters and my son to snatch a peep at the screen, I was gratified to see that Wolves were leading 2–1. It stayed that way to the end, three precious points from Colin Lee's first away win since he'd been appointed manager. Robbie Keane scored in the first minute, capitalising on the Tranmere keeper's disastrous goalkick and Fernando added another in the 12th minute. Tranmere's only goal came after 20 minutes, Santos heading in from a corner. It was a result that made my birthday weekend in Ireland all the sweeter.

My fellow football travellers were quick to point out to me the downside of the game when I got back to Wolverhampton. Ray and Len were agreed that it had been an abysmal performance by Wolves; for David Instone, our midfield had failed to function after we'd scored our goals. Perhaps, we reasoned, there was justice in our theft of the three points; we could all remember the games we had dominated but had lost through the cruelty of chance.

Our last league game before the cup-tie against Arsenal was at Molineux: Graham Taylor was back in town, with his promotion-chasing Watford side. Our respective positions in the league table showed how our fortunes had been reversed since that balmy night in August when our 2–0 win at Vicarage Road had left us on top of the world: Watford were now in sixth place, five places and five points above us. Regardless of his disasters with the English national team, you had to admire Graham Taylor – his team, after all, had only just been promoted out of Division Two and were now challenging for yet another promotion. In the Molineux press room Taylor still had his supporters, hardened hacks who believed that he had not been given enough time to turn Wolves around; Sir Jack himself was quoted in *The Guardian* as saying that 'we should never have let Graham Taylor go'.

The game was wonderfully nondescript: the 0–0 result fairly summed up the exchanges and the penetrative abilities of both sides.

There was one memorable moment. Halfway through the second half Fernando was replaced by the Australian, Steve Corica. Corica is not too tall and he's dark-haired; in the distance, he could be mistaken for David Connolly, who was also on the bench.

He *was* mistaken for Connolly by the Watford travelling fans. To remind him of how unloved he is at Vicarage Road – Connolly had left Watford, going to Ajax, as soon as he was out of contract – the Watford contingent immediately began to chant: 'Connolly's a wanker!'

To which Molineux immediately responded: 'You stupid fucking bastards!'

Well, you have to write something in your notebook on a chilly January afternoon at an unmemorable game.

Yet I err: the day was memorable for two further notable events.

One was the debut of Haavard Flo in a Wolves shirt. He scored no goals but his height and power were like balm for the troubled souls of those among us who had long felt that Robbie needed such a partner up front. The Norwegian visibly tired towards the end but he did enough to give us hope.

The other noteworthy feature of the day was that my picture appeared in the match programme, alongside a brief account of our floodlit, flood-laden excursion to Swindon on Boxing Day. Like every writer, I love to see my words in print but that day was truly special: for a moment I was a boy again, my eyes wide with wonder at the magic of it all – my picture and my words were there among the magic pages of Molineux and nothing, not even a humdrum scoreless draw, could dull the dreaming splendour of the day.

24

Divine Guidance

Len took the wheel the following Saturday for the run up to Stockport. We pulled off the M6 for the usual coffee and a continuation of the analysis that had begun before we'd even left Wolverhampton. We were hopeful: the game against County was the first of a three-match sequence against less-fancied clubs – you simply had to hope for a maximum haul of points from that day's away game and the two subsequent matches, against Oxford and Port Vale, both to be played at Molineux.

Back on the road again, we went astray somewhere in Cheadle. I left the back seat of the car to hail a passing vicar and was rewarded with chapter and verse on the most direct route to Stockport County. 'Definitely not one of ours,' I told Ray and Len when I got back into the car. 'Has to be Anglican, with all that beautiful modulation.' With the divinity to guide us, we had no trouble in reaching the ground; believe it or not, even a parking spot materialised before our eyes, almost directly opposite the main entrance. Moral: never underestimate the power of heaven.

The Stockport County ground is a far cry from the magnificence we have become accustomed to at Molineux. You could almost wish that County would win their way into the Premiership just for the mischievous pleasure of watching the distaste-wrinkled noses of some overpaid 'fancy dans' having to strut their stuff in such humble surroundings. I didn't get to see the dressing-rooms, but if they're anything like the 'Press Tea Room', they'll be small, cramped and distinctly untidy. But – and it's an important 'but' – they'll also be friendly and welcoming.

If I have time, I like to go walkabout in these 'away' towns; more than once I had to pinch myself, realising that dots and names on maps and atlases were alive under my rambling feet; getting a glimpse of shops and pubs and caffs was an important element of my travels. (Sometimes there was nothing to see, as in the neighbourhood of The Hawthorns.)

We were early that Saturday, so I left my two accomplices feverishly hunting for a live phone socket that would allow them to broadcast for Radio Wulfrun and made my personal tour. The area was a bit down-at-heel; I couldn't tell if it had seen better days or if it had always been so and was just waiting for better days to come. The shopping precinct opposite the ground was busy with Saturday shoppers. This was tracksuit-and-trainers country; the shops were full of cheap goods and friendly hope.

I paid 50p for my cuppa – naturally there were no pots – in a caff in the middle of the precinct; the young fellow behind the high zinc counter smiled as he handed me the tea, cheerfully slopping the contents on to the saucer. I grabbed a couple of paper napkins to do a mopping-up job before carefully placing the remains of my cuppa on the red plastic table near the door. I failed to notice that the red table and yellow chairs were one of those all-joined-up-together jobs: when I sat into the chair the entire structure jumped and the newly mopped saucer was once more awash. Some things you can only laugh at . . .

People came and went as I leafed through the match programme. The cover was in a league of its own: a black background covered by an arrangement of white circles. Floodlights, perhaps. Or maybe the printer had misplaced an old snooker cover from the Crucible. Or maybe it was arty and I couldn't see the art.

A policeman stuck his head in the door and waved at the aproned proprietor. Yes, came the shout from the counter, everything was okay. Another constabulary wave, together with a shouted promise to check again later on. Maybe they were expecting Al Capone.

Or Gary Megson.

Minutes before the game was due to start, the Stockport manager raced on to the pitch and grabbed the mike from the match-day compere who was announcing anniversaries, birthdays and winning ticket numbers; microphone in hand, Megson bounded away to my right to address the home kop.

Megson's harangue was like nothing I'd heard anywhere on my footballing travels. For County to stay in Division One, he declared, they needed seven wins from their remaining 18 games – and for that to happen they needed the fans' noisiest support. 'This lot,' Megson went on, gesturing towards the travelling Wolfpack, 'have been in it for the last 14 years and have spent 25 million quid in the process.' The implication was obvious: gallant Stockport were poor but were triers; Wolves had money but could achieve little . . . and the locals should get noisily behind their team. For naked bipartisanship, Megson's performance took the biscuit.

It was also a performance that should have earned County a stuffing. It came out all right in the end but it wasn't quite the magisterial performance I would have loved to see. Wolves began with the same line-up which they had started with the week before against Arsenal. Robbie Keane was again partnered up front by Flo: it seemed ages since that scoreless day in Crewe when Steve Bull had last worn the famous old-gold shirt. Neil Emblen, almost everybody's favourite, was retained in midfield, alongside Robinson, Osborn and Gilkes, who was starting his third consecutive match. Mark Atkins, who had made only one appearance in the season under Mark McGhee, seemed to be making the right-back position his own under Colin Lee's management – Richards, Curle and Muscat gave the back four a settled appearance.

In a bread-and-butter game, we took the lead through a Dean Richards' header from a corner in the tenth minute of the second half. Just two minutes later, in a typical Wolves lapse of concentration, Stockport's dark angel rose to head in the equaliser. This time, however, there would be no repeat of the punning headlines that had followed Brett Angell's two equalising goals against us at Molineux way back in August. On this occasion, the Celestial Director of Football appeared to be on our side: with 15 minutes remaining, Carl Robinson struck a harmless-looking shot towards the County goal, a deflection followed and, almost before I realised what had happened, the ball was in the net. Our deflected good fortune – long overdue, we felt in Wolverhampton – was enough to give us the three points. Maybe the result taught Gary Megson a little lesson, too, in sporting behaviour towards guests at the County ground.

25

'Easy' Games?

After Stockport, Oxford and Port Vale made up the three-game sequence from which many of us felt Wolves had to take maximum points. Both games were played at Molineux.

Oxford came first. Off the field they were having financial troubles that put the continued existence of the club in doubt; on the pitch they weren't doing much better – third from bottom, with only 25 points from 28 games. Out of these 28 games, Oxford had won only six. In other words, their goose was ripe for cooking at Molineux.

And yet Oxford left Wolverhampton that Saturday evening with a precious point. It was a frustrating game. Wolves dominated from the kick-off. As early as the fourth minute, the referee was pronounced a wanker by the locals for letting Gilchrist off with only a yellow card for a heavy challenge on Carl Robinson on the edge of the box. Wolves were passing the ball with sweet precision. Haavard Flo was through but was called back by a very late offside flag. In the tenth minute, Flo was breaking clear when the keeper challenged him, seeming to handle outside the area, but no free kick was given to us.

It was Robbie Keane who put us ahead, after 37 minutes, winning the race for possession with the Oxford goalie and then slotting home from about 20 yards. Moments later, with the ground still buzzing, came the big-screen announcement that West Brom were losing 2–0 away to Sheffield: icing for our old-gold cake!

Three minutes after that it all went wrong. Keith and Deeno were again marked absent, allowing Windass to right-foot the ball high into the net past an angry Stowell. You couldn't blame Mike Stowell for being less than enchanted with his defence. It was a landmark game for Mike: his 350th league appearance for Wolves. His total of 408 appearances for the club meant that he was fast closing on Bert Williams' record of 420 in the Wolves' goalkeeper's jersey.

The game ran away from us after half-time. As Oxford concentrated on protecting their away point, Wolves grew more ragged, unable to break them down. There were boos after the final whistle; I couldn't be sure if they were intended for our players or for the referee.

The other results of the day didn't help our mood. West Brom had been beaten 3–0; Grimsby, Huddersfield, Norwich and Watford had all lost. It was a set of results tailor-made for us, but we had failed to take full advantage of the misfortunes of the other play-off contenders.

Robbie Keane was away in Dublin the week of the Oxford game, leading the Irish attack with Niall Quinn of Sunderland in a friendly against Paraguay. Robbie didn't score in Ireland's 2–0 win but Wolves still got on the scoreboard: David Connolly, coming on as a substitute midway through the second half, scored Ireland's second goal 15 minutes from the end. On that 'international Wednesday' (the same day that England, without Glenn Hoddle and Eileen Drewery, were outclassed by a brilliant French side at Wembley) Haavard Flo was also on international duty, for Norway against Italy. At the same time Carl Robinson was away with the Welsh B squad while Lee Naylor was with the England under-18s.

Such international call-ups demonstrated the rich depth and breadth of the Wolves squad, but it also signalled a looming danger that could imperil our entire promotion challenge. Robbie Keane had been named in Ireland's provisional squad for the World under-20s championships to be held in Nigeria in April, a crucial month when we would be facing a run-in against difficult opposition that included West Brom and Birmingham.

It was patently absurd that Wolves should be deprived of the star player of their senior team for an underage competition. There was nothing 'underage' about Robbie, despite his youth. He needed no fresh stage to demonstrate his abundant talent: he was already doing that, for Wolves and for Ireland. Besides, Wolves pay his wages and the club needed him to sustain their promotion push. Sooner rather than later FIFA must amend its ridiculous rules and exempt senior club players from international call-up for underage competitions.

Wolves, like Leeds, were protesting about these crazy regulations but, as Colin Lee said, their hands were tied.

That February week, however, was brightened by unexpected news. Against all expectations, Steve Bull announced that he would soon be back in training and that he hoped to play again in March. There had been complications following Steve's surgery on his knee after the Crewe game in October; rumour was rampant that Steve was finished. This latest news was a reminder of Bull's indomitable spirit, his determination to give his all for the old-gold and black. Maybe − just maybe, I hoped − the king would be fit enough to take his place for those crucial games in April, when our crown prince would be absent in Nigeria. If only that old Celestial Director would lend an ear to my promptings . . .

★

The Newbridge training ground was a cold, frosty place that international Wednesday morning. I rambled on to the ground, as was my weekly custom, at about half-past eleven. John Ward, standing alongside the Gaffer, gave me a friendly wave; training had only just started, John told me, they'd been waiting for the frozen ground to thaw out.

When I arrived, Keith Curle was conducting a non-taxing running session on one of the pitches. Keith, probably coming to the end of his playing days, was now also easing himself into a coaching role at Wolves. Beside me, watching the double file of players warming up, John was laughing. 'Look at the old pros,' he said, 'taking it carefully on the hard ground while the youngsters are killing themselves.'

There was a handful of new young faces in the group. Normally the youngsters trained separately on the upper pitch at the top of the bank, but this morning a few of them had been drafted in to make up the numbers in place of our international absentees. Giving the youngsters a chance to train occasionally with the seniors was something John and

Colin Lee were keen on: it was part of a familiarisation process, getting them used to stronger opponents and also to the occasional chastisement of older hands who did not suffer incompetence gladly.

Something else struck me about the morning: there was a kind of resentful sullenness in the atmosphere as if the players were not too keen on being here, with their panting breath hanging like gunsmoke in the freezing air. Did some of them, I asked John, feel that they should be having a day off when their international team-mates were away?

John grinned. Yes, he said, one of the senior players — he named him but I prefer to leave him unnamed here — had come looking for a day off. 'I told him and the rest of them,' John said, 'that he wasn't as good as Robbie Keane and the others. Robbie was training on Monday before flying to Dublin, he trained yesterday with the Irish squad and he'll play tonight, fly back tomorrow, train on Friday and play against Port Vale on Saturday. He's better than you and he's doing all his training and playing and you want a day off!'

John spoke with good-humoured irony, but I could detect in his words the steeliness which had to be part of the coaching character: our gaffer, I figured, had chosen well for his number two.

After John put the squad through some speedy touch-passing movements, Colin took over for a full-width, half-length match session. He had his bits of paper ready with line-ups; from time to time he'd refer to them, switching personnel, altering shapes — the gaffer had done his own homework. The mood lifted. The frosty air rang with the shouts of players, with the thwack of boot on ball. The gaffer's big, loud voice encouraged and cajoled, called back and urged on. His team responded to his loud urgings, as they always seemed to do: nobody could doubt the difference Colin had made.

I loved it, standing there in that wide expanse of green, watching, listening, just being there. Beyond the boundary of high trees and tennis courts lay the ordinary world of traffic and mortgages and appointments, but in the grassy enclave the morning was brushed with magic and I was content to be there . . .

Even the presence of Steve Bull and Steve Froggatt hadn't been enough to save us from a humiliating defeat at Port Vale early in September: we'd gone into that game as joint leaders with Sunderland while Vale had been bottom of the table. For the return game at Molineux, therefore, there was something of a score to settle. Mostly, I think, Wolves had a score to settle with themselves rather than with the opposition: we had dominated that Tuesday evening game, but Port Vale had won through two opportunist breakaway goals.

Looking down at the sideline that Saturday afternoon, you couldn't help but reflect on the cruel uncertainties of a footballing life. Colin Lee had replaced Mark McGhee in our dugout; the much admired John Rudge had been forced, after 14 years at the Vale helm, to give way to Brian Horton.

There were changes in our on-the-field line-up too. Michael Gilkes was dropped, after four consecutive starts, and Paul Simpson was starting in a league game for the first time in the season.

It was Simpson who put us in front in the third minute, his angled shot going in off the upright. Molineux was on its feet: this kind of flying start was exactly what we wanted. Two minutes later the unthinkable — or inevitable? — happened. A slack clearance from Deeno found its way to the boot of Vale's Ian Bogie; Bogie shot, but he was over 20 yards out, and his shot seemed to have no great power behind it; the ball bounced in front of Mike Stowell and then, inexplicably, ended up in our net.

Well might Mike hang his head. Yet I could only feel sorry for his uncharacteristic lapse. I knew how hard he worked, how much of himself he pumped into endless sessions at the training ground. I'd stand on the bank behind his goal and watch him and Matt Murray, his young understudy, go through one gruelling sequence after another — shots from the right, from the left; shots from in front; shots high and low. I'd never had a conversation with him; we'd just exchange 'good mornings' and he'd say 'thank you' whenever I went off to fetch an errant ball. Now, looking down at Mike from the Billy Wright stand, I could only share his misery. I just hoped it wouldn't affect his confidence too much.

Robbie Keane put us ahead again, just after the half-hour. Sedgley delivered a long through ball and Robbie pounced, sliding the ball home with his right foot.

Half-time came and went without further scores. But there were goals at the Reebok: in the 13th minute of the second half, Molineux cheered the TV announcement that West Brom were losing 2–1 away to Bolton. Some ten minutes later Flo and Robinson were replaced by David

Connolly and Neil Emblen, and Wolves piled on the pressure. Vale held out until a minute from time: Robbie went down in the box and Keith Curle made no mistake with the penalty.

The 3–1 victory put us firmly back in the frame for the play-offs: we were now in seventh place, just a single point behind sixth-placed Watford. Our three-game 'easy' sequence against Stockport, Oxford and Vale had not yielded the nine points we had all craved, but seven out of nine was not a haul you'd be complaining about. Small wonder that Colin Lee and John Ward arrived for the post-match press conference with smiles on their faces and half-full champagne glasses in their hands . . .

26
'A Few Broken Hearts'

It's a long run from Wolverhampton up to Sunderland. It was just after eight o'clock that Saturday morning when my travelling companions collected me on Tettenhall Road. The morning was chilly but bright; we made good time, heading up the spine of England, along the A38 and then on to the M1. We had the usual pit stop somewhere north of Darlington. Over cardboard cups of coffee we discussed, with our usual optimism, the ramifications of the day's programme – anyone would think, listening to us, that we had not lost an away game all season; that it was Wolves, not Sunderland, who were running a separate solo race at the top of the table.

Sunderland had opened up an eight-point gap on the rest of us; Wolves stood on 48 points, a colossal 18 points behind them. We all realised that our only chance now lay in making the play-offs: we had to finish in the top six. Our cause would be helped should our immediate rivals for the sixth spot stumble, especially Watford, who had two points more than us, and Grimsby who, like ourselves, had 48 points. That Saturday, Grimsby were away to Barnsley while Watford were travelling to Loftus Road to face Queen's Park Rangers.

The day turned colder as we swung east, south of Newcastle. We could see the Stadium of Light ahead of us: a bowl of off-white metal set on top of a ring of dark red brick, the whole structure rooted in a black half-finished expanse of mucky earth and builder's materials. It's a Premiership ground: a full house – and Sunderland often have them – is around 42,000. Attendances at the Stadium of Light had always soared beyond any other in the First Division; even Molineux, all golden dreams and gleaming loos, lagged some 15,000 behind.

And yet, for me, the stadium itself soared neither into the sky nor beyond my imagination. Its facilities were enviable – the spacious press room at Sunderland would make a lovely venue for a series of chamber music concerts – and the folk who live there are as friendly and hospitable as you could hope to meet in a long season of travelling, but the ground itself, seen from the outside, lacks the soaring elegance of the Reebok at Bolton or the McAlpine at Huddersfield.

It was undoubtedly the noisiest ground I had been to: the din as the teams emerged could have shattered eardrums. On Hughie Green's old clapometer Sunderland would, by now, have already won the championship.

I didn't fear them. Nor did most of the Wolves fans I spoke to. Only a 94th-minute goal had deprived us of a win over Sunderland at Molineux back in September; besides, Wolves folk always feel that the boys in the old-gold and black play better against good-quality opposition. And here we were meeting quality: in 31 league games to date, Sunderland had lost only one game at the Stadium of Light (3–2 against Barnsley in November), while they had been beaten on the road only by Tranmere (1–0 on Boxing Day) and Watford (2–1 in late January).

Wolves began confidently. In the very first minute Robbie was brought down on the edge of the area by Makin but the free kick produced nothing. You could sense the team settling to their task when disaster struck: Johnston was allowed a free run into our box and put a low shot under Mike Stowell and into our net. On the pitch the celebrations seemed muted – one reporter had told me there was ill-feeling among some of the Sunderland players – but the fans would have lifted the roof had the stadium had one.

A couple of minutes later, Robbie broke through the Sunderland defence on his own but his attempt at placing the ball wide of Sorensen was easily saved by the keeper. Muscat ankle-tapped Quinn: the free kick was given but no card was brandished. Minutes later the Australian crossed from the left, Flo headed it on but again Robbie's shot was saved. Robbie returned the favour in the next minute, touching the ball on for Muscat but his shot was again safety dealt with by Sorensen.

We were back in the hunt in the 23rd minute. Simon Osborn's long ball into the box fell between Robbie Keane and Melville and somehow the Sunderland man contrived to put the ball past his own keeper. It was a personal disaster for the unfortunate Melville: in the same fixture the year before he had also delivered an own-goal to Wolves. Not that the Wolfpack behind the goal on my right were offering any sympathy: we had ourselves been too often on the receiving end of misfortune.

Lady Luck – or the referee – set his or her face against us in the second half. Twice in the space of four minutes, Robbie had the ball in the Sunderland net, but on both occasions he was whistled back – the second time for 'arming' the ball, the first for nothing that was apparent to me or anyone I desperately quizzed.

By then Peter Reid was on his feet, his balled, waving fist almost punching his men forward into renewed attack. For the last 25 minutes of the match the Stadium of Light became a hostile cauldron of noise as the red-and-white army urged on The Lads. These lads, in such a setting, were always likely to get the winner. Yet attack after attack was repulsed; minute after minute ticked away, and still we held out. No Spartan defended the Pass of Thermopylae with more courage and determination than Wolves showed on that bitterly cold afternoon in the north-east. When, finally, our citadel was breached, it was by ill-luck that we were undone. In the 92nd minute, in the middle of what the late Michael O'Hehir would have called 'a schemozzle in the goalmouth', the ball went loose, scooting across the front of our goal, and it was a Sunderland boot that got to it first, belting it past a helpless Mike Stowell into our net.

Inevitably, it had to be an Irishman who delivered that *coup de grâce*: Niall Quinn, predator and Irishman, had done it again.

I was sitting near the front when Niall came in for the post-match press conference.

'A terrible man,' I said, loudly enough for him to hear.

Niall doesn't know me from Adam, but he recognised the accent.

He flashed a big smile. 'Did I spoil your headlines?'

I wanted to tell him that it was my life he was spoiling, but I held my peace. He's a charming fellow, Niall Quinn, and has done the football state some service in Ireland. Even in the depths of my misery and prejudice I could see that he had just been doing his job. I didn't want to see it – but I could. Just.

Colin Lee was trying to be philosophical after the game, but you could see the hurt in the brave smile. Nobody could be blamed for the goal, he said, every man jack in the Wolves team had played his heart out. It was hard to take, he said, remembering that they had done it to us at Molineux as well.

'Is everyone okay?' someone asked. 'Any injuries?'

'No,' Colin answered, 'but there's a few broken hearts in that dressing-room right now.'

Mine too, I thought, just a bit choked by the unaccustomed tenderness of Colin's words. I'd stood on the sideline at the training ground often enough to know that Colin's good looks and affable manner concealed a core of steel and determination; this gentleness was unexpected – it was almost as if my sergeant-major father had suddenly begun to quote Yeats's love lyrics in that time, long ago, back in Galway.

The long journey in the darkness back to Wolverhampton was strangely upbeat. We hadn't a point to show for our travels, but we were proud of our team. Not a man among them had let the side down. Only misfortune had laid us low, like a stray bullet ricocheting among the rocks. From now on, we figured, we were surely safe from such accursed lightning.

27

Lightning Strikes Twice

We should have known better.

A week later, back at Molineux on the last Saturday in February, another bullet ricocheted among the rocks. Or maybe we just shot ourselves in the foot.

Huddersfield were the opposition. They no longer topped the table as they had, back in September, when yet another last-gasp goal had beaten us 2–1, but they were still in the chase for the play-offs.

We had their measure early on. Only 11 minutes had passed when we were in front: Robbie's angled shot was parried by the keeper but Carl Robinson, racing on to the clearance, belted the ball into the net. It was the kind of start that Wolves needed in their 2,000th home league game, but they failed to increase their lead in that first half, despite their supremacy. Fourteen minutes into the second half we gave away our hard-earned advantage: Kevin Gray, the Huddersfield captain, got on the end of a diagonal cross from Baldry and headed low into our net.

We were still shaking our heads a few minutes later when, to the delight of Wolves and the horror of our visitors, the luckless Gray scored again – this time his attempt at a headed clearance of a Simon Osborn cross gave Vaesen no chance in the Huddersfield goal. You couldn't tell where you stood with that old Celestial Director: it was our second gifted own-goal in as many games. This time, surely, we'd make sure to hang on to our lead.

Robbie Keane had to go off midway through the second half with a shoulder injury – not serious, we were relieved to learn later – and he seemed to take with him the heart of the team. Wolves sat back and Huddersfield kept rolling forward. High up in the stand I kept thinking: we're doing it again, we're going to do it again . . .

We were still in front when the 90 minutes were up and the sign went up for just one minute of extra time. Huddersfield went on attacking, Wolves kept hoofing the ball clear and each time it came right back at them.

There was a brutal inevitability about the goal. It came in the second minute of extra time when Hamilton booted the ball in. Our hearts sank. What had we done to deserve these last-minute body-blows? Or what had we not done?

Colin Lee admitted after the game that he didn't know what was wrong. If he discovered it, he said, he'd put it right.

Thinking it over in the days that followed, I figured I knew what Colin didn't. Our team had shared in the dread and expectation that had gripped us in the stands – the awful certainty that a late goal was inevitable. Both players and supporters needed to start believing all over again that we were good enough to win games.

We also needed Kevin Muscat back. I'd spoken briefly to Kevin before the kick-off: his arm was in a sling, his hand in plaster, a number of bones inside broken in an accidental collision with Robbie Keane. It had seemed harmless at the time, he said, but the surgeon had told him he could expect to be out of the game for five or six weeks. It was not an encouraging note on which to end the month of February. There was, however, a last saving grace: Steve Bull was back in training and would feature in a reserve game early in March against Bolton. Maybe, just maybe, his coming would lead us to the promised land.

28

'An Outside Chance'

As February turned to March, I took my own soundings in the Molineux press room. My straw poll had two questions: (a) are we going to make the play-offs, and (b) will Colin Lee be manager of Wolves next season? Of the half-dozen or so journalists I put my questions to, not a man among them – females of the sports journalist species are still rare sightings, more's the pity – thought that Wolves would make the play-offs; it followed, naturally, that Molineux would have a new manager the following season.

You couldn't ignore the opinions of these seasoned scribes. Molineux was their 'beat', for dailies, for weeklies, for radio stations. They were immersed in the minutiae of the club – the comings and goings, injuries and recoveries, fact and gossip. They all had their own personal footballing loyalties – one of them even supported Chester City – but I sensed that all of them wished Wolves well. It wasn't merely that promotion would also upgrade the journalists themselves to Premiership status, although that too would have been welcome; it was more, I think, that fellows get sucked into the lives of the players and back-room staff whom they have interviewed so often. When you get to know folk, you want them to do well.

Of course, I couldn't agree with them about Wolves' prospects. I saw things differently: I was a fan among them. David Instone merely smiled whenever I offered my pre-match prediction; my forecast was always the same, he told me, and it never included a draw or a defeat. Ian Willars constantly reminded me that in the press room I must always refer to Wolves in the third person, never as 'we'; the Duke's rebukes – always gracious – taught me to sit on my hands in the press box, even when *we* were working magic on the pitch.

Colin Lee saw things differently too. A couple of days before the Huddersfield game I'd fallen into step beside Colin as he followed his players off the training ground. He warned me – correctly as it turned out – that Huddersfield were an able side; he spoke fondly of Terry Yorath, Peter Jackson's assistant at Huddersfield, who'd been a team-mate of Colin's at Spurs.

We had reached the car-park when I put my question.

'So what d'you make of it now, Colin?'

'Of what?'

'Our chances of making the play-offs.'

'I think we have an outside chance,' Colin said. 'We're in much better shape now than when I took over – yes, we're in with an outside chance.'

Colin was slipping out of his football boots into a pair of sandals for the drive back to Molineux when I left him. My good wishes weren't enough to win us the three points against Huddersfield – if good wishes could work, we'd be in the Champions League by now – but at least the draw, however unpalatable it tasted at the time, had kept us in the hunt. On Monday, 1 March, the top of the table looked like this:

Place	Team	Played	Points
1.	Sunderland	33	70
2.	Bradford	33	61
3.	Ipswich	33	61
4.	Bolton	32	59
5.	Birmingham	33	57
6.	Watford	34	53
7.	Wolves	33	49
8.	Grimsby	32	49
9.	West Brom	34	47
10.	Norwich	32	47

Behind us only on goals scored, Grimsby had a game in hand, but on that last weekend in February they had been thrashed 3–0 at home by Birmingham, which would have done little for their confidence. Watford had also lost at home on that same weekend, 1–0 against Swindon: we didn't know it then but Watford were beginning an expensive losing streak. As Colin had said, we were in with an outside chance.

The schedule of games for the first fortnight in March also gave us hope: our four games, including two Tuesday night matches, were against four teams from the bottom six of the table: Bury (22nd), Queen's Park Rangers (19th), Crewe Alexandra (24th and bottom) and Bristol City (23rd).

I set my face against both hacks and fans who said Wolves invariably tripped up against lowly opposition. We needed a full haul from these games, I told myself, and anyone who bothered to listen: twelve points from four games. The only way to go, I added needlessly, was onwards and upwards.

29

Nothing Doing at Bury

My rendezvous with Gerry for the Bury game was just off the M6, at Junction 10, just before noon. Gerry didn't push the big Lexus: kick-off wasn't until 7.45 p.m. Gerry's twenty-something son, Matthew, was in the back along with his mate, Nick. The conversation – of course it was about football – was as unhurried as our progress along the motorway. Nobody paid much attention to the gentle Black Country rain.

Nor did we pay too much attention to it up in Blackburn. Gerry managed to park close to the supermarket entrance and we had only a short dash across the car-park for a quick Tesco lunch. Business at Gerry's head office in Blackburn seemed to involve as much socialising as anything else: hands were shaken, banter exchanged, boxes and documents stowed in the boot. Then we were off again, this time to Burnley.

St Joseph's Convent in Burnley has been home, for the last year or so, to my Aunt Mary. Mary is my father's sister, the last surviving member of her generation; since my mother and all of her siblings have died, Mary is, in fact, the last member of my clan from the generations born before me. She has given her life to the Franciscan sisterhood, spending her nun's life almost entirely abroad – in the USA and in Ecuador. Radiotherapy for cancer had brought her from the States to this convent in Burnley for elderly and infirm sisters.

My aunt, I think, had a notion of making a missionary priest out of me when I was a boy. That didn't happen, but ever since then I have loved this tiny aunt of mine with the gentle ways and the soft voice. It was good to dash through the Burnley rain, heavier now, and in through the back door of the convent, into the kitchen, and find Mary well and smiling and getting into her usual dither about whether to welcome us or to go off immediately to make tea for us.

If you let it happen, a place like a convent will seep into your soul. A kind of contentment, born of praying lips and fingered beads, settles upon you. The world doesn't go away but seen from the quiet confines of a prayerful place, it grows less threatening, more wonderful. We absorbed that contentment, along with the tea and the chat and the biscuits. Mary showed Gerry and myself around the building – Matthew and Nick had gone to the pub – and we knelt for a few minutes in the convent oratory. The sanctuary lamp glowed red and dim; a few sisters were rapt in their devotion. The world almost did go away.

And then we were back into it, racing across the yard to the car in the now pelting rain. My aunt waved; I heard her call out that she'd say a prayer for us in the match.

Even my Aunt Mary's prayers couldn't stop the rain. Just after five, as we were pushing on towards Bury, we heard on the car radio that the game had been called off.

Yet in a way we were still winners on the night. Watford lost further ground, going down 3–2 away to Ipswich. Huddersfield's 3–2 home win over Bolton had hauled them alongside us on 49 points but they had played a game more than us. The Baggies had also won at home, beating Stockport 3–1, and so leap-frogging above us on to 50 points – we had, however, two games in hand of them. West Brom were, therefore, not to be written off as yet. I remembered how Nick, contemplating a Lord Denning-like 'appalling vista' of a Baggies promotion on the journey to Bury, had consoled himself with the thought that he'd 'have the pleasure of watching them go right back down again next season'.

At half past ten that night, after getting the results, I called Gerry at his home in Sutton Coldfield to compare notes. Despite the cancellation of the game, it had been a good day; we had not lost ground against any of our serious opponents for that crucial sixth-place play-off position. Maybe the old CDF had, after all, been listening to Aunt Mary's prayers.

30

Bully's Road Back

The night of 3 March 1999 was bitterly cold in the Black Country: frost was glinting on the pavements and on the bare branches of the trees around my flat on Tettenhall Road. It was a night when it would take something special to draw you out from your fireside and your TV. (Manchester United were on the box, playing a European gig, which might also be considered a stay-at-home attraction for some citizens of blinkered vision.)

Yet some 8,500 besotted men, women and children braved the frosty night to welcome back their local hero. A reserve game against Bolton Wanderers was the chosen vehicle for Steve Bull's competitive come-back, five months to the day since he'd last lined out against Crewe, way back in October. When Bully, accompanied by a couple of young mascots, led Wolves out on to the Molineux turf, the crowd rose to him in a standing ovation. His come-back on that soggy, wintry pitch was confirmation yet again of Bull's indomitable spirit and his commitment to the old-gold and black.

We watched with bated breath to see how the fragile knee would hold up. I'd watched Steve the week before on the Newbridge training pitch and I had marvelled at the commitment of the man: Keith Curle had supervised a sprinting session which had left the players on their hunkers, gasping for breath in the frosty morning. Bully, too, had been on his knees after those lung-bursting sprints, but he had not spared himself; neither had he lagged behind players who were ten and more years younger than he was. That morning the talk of crutches and wheelchairs had seemed like malicious, unfounded gossip.

This frosty night at Molineux was different. Tougher, more demanding questions would be asked of Steve and his rebuilt knee. There would be no 'excuse me's from the Bolton professionals; no tackle would be shirked on the soggy pitch. So we waited and watched and hoped.

Bull was playing alongside David Connolly up front; behind him young Shane Tudor flanked an international midfield of Fernando, Corica and Niestroj. Welsh international Ryan Green was at the back along with the youngsters Haveron and Lescott and the Northern Ireland Under-18 player, Gordon Simms. Mike Stowell's young understudy, Matt Murray, was in goal.

The Bolton side was full of Viking 'sons' – Kristianson, Bergsson, Neilsen, Hansen, Morrison (sorry!); it also included the Jamaican World Cup player, Ricardo Gardner.

Despite all the youthful and international talent on display; all eyes were focused on Bully. From the start, he held nothing back, even foraging deep in search of the ball. In the 28th minute we got – almost – what we wanted: standing to the left of the Bolton goal, Bully trapped, turned and shot in a single, swivelling movement . . . the ball went wide, but the crowd was happy. God still knew where the net was; he just needed a little practice. Hansen, a £1 million buy from Brondby, put Bolton ahead soon after that but, three minutes before the interval, Corica laid a nice ball through to Bull; Steve's on-target effort was parried by the keeper but Robert Niestroj was on hand to tap in the equaliser.

About a quarter of an hour remained when Bully came off. Once more the ground rose to him. There was relief in the air: as far as we could see, that fragile, precious knee had come through the fire intact.

Amid the heartfelt applause for Bully's departure, most of the crowd might not have paid too much attention to his replacement. I did: it was none other than my young townsman, Seamus Crowe. I told the Duke, sitting beside me, to make a note of it: it took a Galwayman to fill the space left by a Molineux legend. I wondered if Seamus himself realised the significance of the moment.

I asked him just that a few days later in the Molineux reception area, when I was handing over my week-old copy of The Connacht Tribune.

Seamus just smiled his freckled, Irish smile. 'Nobody,' he said, 'can replace Bully.'

Bolton had won the game 3–1, but the real winners were Wolverhampton: Bully was on the way back.

31

Escape from Loftus Road

You don't get to see much of London on the run in to Loftus Road. You head in along the A40, easing off the dual carriageway at White City – you mustn't take the flyover on to the Westway – turning right on to Wood Lane and then right again into South Africa Road. You can see the blue-and-grey stadium of Queen's Park Rangers ahead of you, at the end of the street. It's easy-peasy, compared with the tortuous snaking journey you have to make through the suburbs of south London to get to Selhurst Park.

Ray and myself talked our way into some official-looking car-park a goal-kick from the main entrance. We were only two that day – Len was on compassionate leave, attending some family anniversary celebration. We had tendered our sympathies.

That first Saturday in March was a bitterly cold day, with a biting wind whipping through the streets of Shepherd's Bush. While Ray was checking out his radio plugs and thingummies, I took refuge in the press room. It was a lively place, with plenty of chat and cheer: Londoners like to gab as much as the Irish. They might keep to themselves on the streets and on the Tube, but put them into a football setting and their tongues flap with ease. Someone pointed out to me with some glee that Wolves hadn't won at Loftus Road since December 1967. 'Mind you,' he added tartly, 'for a lot of those years we weren't in the same Division.' I needed no reminding that our only home defeat in the present campaign had been inflicted on us the previous September by QPR.

That game at Loftus Road on 6 March was, for me, one of the most memorable of the season. The football was neither elegant nor pretty, but it was full-blooded and passionate. Both sides needed the points — Wolves, to haul themselves into play-off contention; QPR, to lift themselves clear of the trapdoor to Division Two.

My recollection of the game is highlighted by a handful of key incidents but mostly what I remember is the atmosphere of the afternoon. Loftus Road is a compact, intimate ground; when the crowd gets behind their team — as they did that freezing day — it is also incredibly hostile to visitors. These supporters hurled both praise and insults alike with a kind of venom that I had not felt at Molineux nor elsewhere on my travels.

The early exchanges were even. Gallen forced a corner for the Rangers on the left, but Emblen headed clear. In the seventh minute, Simpson was well wide with a long-range, speculative shot. Three minutes later, at the end of an intricate Wolves passing movement, Flo was wide with a header. We held our breath another three minutes after that when Kulcsar, an Australian import, accepted a pass from Steiner but his powerful long-range drive was left and wide.

Two of the defining moments of the game came in quick succession.

In the 20th minute, Paul Ready, who had been persistently niggling Haavard Flo, was given a yellow card for yet another foul on the big Norwegian. It was a card that was to have disastrous consequences in the second half.

A minute later, Robbie Keane missed a sitter. Micklosko, the Rangers keeper, attempting to clear a back-pass, completely miskicked and the ball landed at the feet of an unmarked Robbie Keane on the edge of the square . . . Robbie, surely astonished by such a gift, swung with uncharacteristic haste but succeeded only in pushing the ball wide. It was an incredible miss from our genie of Molineux. Maybe he was unbalanced when the ball reached him; Colin Lee would say afterwards that Robbie was off-colour due to the jabs and medications he was having in preparation for the Under-20 business in Nigeria.

By my watch it was 29 minutes before the referee was declared a wanker. The declaration was chanted with growling Loftus Road venom. The occasion was the awarding of a free kick five yards outside the QPR area for a foul on Robbie. Simpson's shot yielded nothing.

A couple of minutes later Robbie was fouled again, dribbling across the edge of the box. Simpson's free kick was deflected for a corner. A second corner followed immediately but again nothing came of it. Wolves were having the better of the exchanges but the sides were still level when the half-time whistle blew.

Eleven minutes after the restart, everything about referee Mathieson – his parentage, his sexual proclivities, his eyesight and his hearing – was questioned by the incensed Loftus Road crowd. Mr Mathieson waved a second yellow card at Ready for another foul on Flo, who was lying stretched out on the pitch, followed by a red card, and the Rangers were down to ten men. Flo left the pitch for a minute or so; when he limped back, the cheers and jeers seemed to come from every windswept street in the Bush. Loftus Road was simply seething with anger.

Ten-man QPR fought their way back into the game, particularly down the left wing, where the teenager Leon Jeanne was giving Mark Atkins a torrid time. Once more Wolves seized the initiative, but time was running out on us.

The half-time news from elsewhere had been mixed: Albion, a point above us before kick-off, had been leading Oxford 1–0, while Watford, also a point above us, had been losing 2–0 away to Sheffield. We needed a goal if we were not to lose further ground to the Baggies.

Two minutes turned the game. Seven minutes from time Mark Atkins was given his marching orders for deliberately kicking at Jeanne. Loftus Road cheered his departure.

They didn't cheer a minute later, when Steve Sedgley courageously dived into the thick of things to head home an incisive cross from Michael Gilkes.

One–nil with just minutes to go! The Wolfpack behind the goal on my right was in seventh heaven. For once that contrary old Celestial Director was not frowning on us.

I'm sure I wasn't the only one on the edge of my seat for those last frantic minutes. There was, as we knew too well, still time for us to throw it away. The Rangers forced two corners as they piled on the pressure, roared on by the crowd, but this time the defence was not found wanting. The three points belonged to Wolves – and deservedly so.

It was no wonder that Colin Lee and John Ward rushed on to the pitch after the final whistle to congratulate each and every one of the eleven – well, ten anyway! – who had carried the day.

Loftus Road was unforgiving: referee Mathieson left the pitch to loud, concerted chanting about his sexual preferences . . .

32

Into the Frame

Wolves had a mid-week evening game at Molineux, against Crewe, scheduled for 9 March. It began to snow in Wolverhampton that Tuesday afternoon at about half past three. It still hadn't stopped by five o'clock. Through the thick grey curtain of falling snow you could hardly see the sky but the writing on the wall was clearly visible. When I phoned Molineux, I got the news I expected: the game was off.

The cancellation held obvious implications – not just a backlog of games piling up but, most probably, one more game to be added to the list which Robbie Keane would miss because of the Nigerian affair.

The game at Bury had been a victim the previous week of rain; it seemed unjust to lose a second one so soon after to snow. Maybe a cyclone – or a heatwave – would claim the game fixed for the following Saturday, when Bristol City were due at Molineux.

The club brought in huge hot-air machines and an enormous, pitch-size plastic cover to ensure that Molineux was playable. We would read later, in the programme, about what the cancellation had cost the club, but few supporters would shed any tears about the expenditure. Colin Lee had repeatedly said that he had no money – and he *meant* no money – to spend on players. The Scrooge-like bra was still padlocked around the golden tit and we could only wonder whether it would be removed even if we did manage to make it into the Premiership. Haavard Flo had cost some £700,000 but Steve Froggatt had gone to Coventry for £2 million, Dougie Freedman to Forest for £900,000 and Steve Claridge to Portsmouth for £200,000. The income from these sales, we were told, had gone to reduce the club overdraft; even the £75,000 Hibernian had paid for Mixu Paatelainen had helped . . .

We'd paid £350,000 to bring in Robert Niestroj, a right-sided midfielder from Fortuna Dusseldorf, but apart from that trickle, the fountain was sealed.

Niestroj had arrived at Molineux in November; he'd been on the bench a few times but hadn't started a game until late December, against Ipswich. That game, together with the cup victory over Bolton and the away match against Stockport, were his only starting appearances.

As luck would have it, it was Robert Neistroj I bumped into at the training ground the day after the snow cancellation. I worked at my desk/table all that morning but the sun was shining and I was in need of a football fix so I took off, rather late, for Newbridge. Most of the players had left: through the screens of trees, beyond the tennis courts, I could see a handful of players gathered in listening pose.

Robert Niestroj is an engaging, intelligent young man – that much was obvious to me as soon as I introduced myself and shook hands with him. For a quarter of an hour he spoke in fluent English about the life he had left behind in Germany and about his new career in Wolverhampton. Wolverhampton was pleasant, he said, but there was more to do in Dusseldorf; it wasn't possible for his girlfriend to join him in England. Most evenings he stayed at home in Tettenhall: he had German TV on cable, he said with a smile. It was, for me, a glimpse of the reality of the much-envied lifestyle of today's successful young footballers. It's a life that brings with it its own peculiar demons, as Stan Collymore and Paul Merson would attest; I suspect that loneliness is a familiar companion for many of these wealthy young athletes in the long stretches between games and training sessions.

Niestroj, it seems to me, has the temperament to deal with such demons. His fluency in English suggests a basic intelligence and a solid educational background that will always be to his advantage. How many of our overpaid Premiership youngsters would cope so well in a foreign tongue and an alien environment?

He spoke frankly about his dislike for playing where the manager wanted him to play.

'Colin wants me to play on the right, in midfield, in 4–4–2,' Robert said, 'but I don't like playing there. I prefer to play in the middle.'

He went on to analyse for me the differences between 4–4–2 and the German formation he preferred. They play 2–3 at the back and midfield, he said, giving you more time on the ball; there's more passing up front with less knocking in of high crosses and centres.

'And have you told Colin this?' I asked.

'Of course.' Niestroj spoke with that frank directness that I have grown used to on my teaching excursions to Germany. In Ireland, we'd broach a subject from half a dozen different directions, terrified lest we'd cause umbrage even to our listener's first cousin, twice removed, on the mother's side. Teutonic directness is alien to us. Maybe we have much to learn from each other.

I find much to admire in these young footballing mercenaries. It's easy to denigrate them, like Yanks in wartime Britain – oversexed, overpaid and over here. In them, as in those GIs of long ago, there's a lot of good stuff, especially the ones like Robert Niestroj.

Haavard Flo is another. I'd managed to have a chat with Flo back in January, not long after his arrival at Molineux. It was the day of the press reception held a few days before the cup-tie against Arsenal. While the hot shots from the national press were feverishly clustered around 'starlet' Robbie Keane, Flo was sitting alone at the end of a long table, tucking contentedly into a plateful of Molineux sandwiches – he's a strapping lad, our Flo, and he needs his sustenance. He was the soul of graciousness when I introduced myself and sat down beside him. Yes, he said, he thought he was going to like it at Wolves, although he did miss Bremen – the city was spotless, with plenty of cafés to sit at in the evenings . . . his few words conjured up an image of a cosmopolitan café-society, far removed from the Black Country.

I was curious about his command of languages – yes, I know I should have asked him more about football, but I'm also a teacher and a writer!

English was from school, Flo said, nearly everybody learned it in Norway. And German? Had he also learned German at school? No, was the answer. Haavard Flo had spoken no German at the start of his two-and-a-half year stint in Germany but he'd taken lessons and had mastered the language. It was the kind of intelligence and commitment, I felt, that would serve Wolves well.

Flo had gone on to score his first goal for Wolves in that cup-tie but had not yet managed to get his name on a league score sheet. As the ground crew at Molineux laboured with might and main to save the Bristol game, you could only hope that Flo's day would not be long in coming.

The game against Bristol went ahead but I had never seen Molineux looking so peculiar. Huge areas of the pitch were covered in yellow sand, like grotesque anti-nicotine patches on withered green flesh.

Half an hour before the kick-off, John Ward made his way across our wounded pitch to the travelling army of Bristol fans in the lower deck of the John Ireland stand. For John it was an emotional moment: in November he had been forced out of his manager's post with such abruptness that there had not been time to say goodbye to friends, fans and colleagues. In one of the game's ever-recurring ironies, Bristol had been trounced 6–1 in the week of John Ward's departure by a Wolves side that was being managed, for the first time, by Colin Lee. John himself had told me how, a few weeks later, he'd phoned Colin Lee on spec. to offer his services at Molineux. 'If you don't ask,' John had said to me, 'you can't win.'

Now here he was, on the Wolves' management team, crossing the patched-up Molineux turf, to say farewell to people he had grown to love over his many years with Bristol. The red army of Bristol had a special place in their hearts for John – you could tell that by the way they rose and applauded him when he stood before them and waved to them. He moved along their front now and I felt a bit of a lump in my throat as I watched the hands reach out to shake his. At such moments, you are reminded that, behind the loot and the greed, football still has a heart and it sometimes wears it on its sleeve. John Ward was most definitely on Wolves' side, but that didn't mean he had to turn his back on the good times he'd shared at Bristol.

We needed to win this one. On that Saturday, 13 March, our section of the table looked like this:

Place	Team	Played	Points
6.	West Brom	36	53
7.	Huddersfield	36	53
8.	Watford	36	53
9.	Wolves	34	52

Albion were at Birmingham that day, while Huddersfield were away to Ipswich, and Watford were at Oxford. The mathematics were simple. If we won and the other results went our way, we could vault into that precious sixth-place, play-off position.

It was Haavard Flo's day. Paul Simpson struck a long, diagonal centre into the Bristol goalmouth and Flo, stretching, managed to get his toe to the ball to poke it into the corner of the net. We were a goal up after a quarter of an hour. The sky was darkening with the threat of rain and the afternoon was growing colder – but the meteorology didn't matter. We were on course for the three points we desperately wanted.

Just 13 minutes later, Flo headed the ball into the Bristol net again, but the referee called play back for pushing in the box. The Wolfpack were so content with the progress of the game that they didn't even bother to denigrate the referee's handiwork.

We had failed to increase our lead by half-time but the news from elsewhere was exactly what we wanted to hear. The Baggies were a goal down to The Blues, Huddersfield were two-down against Ipswich and Sheffield were also losing by two goals at Tranmere.

Five minutes into the second half came the most bizarre goal of the season at Molineux. Volmos Seebok, Bristol's Hungarian defender, tapped a harmless back-pass to his keeper, Steve Phillips; the keeper, a couple of yards off his line and under absolutely no pressure, somehow contrived to nudge the ball goalwards and we watched, open-mouthed, as the ball trickled into the Bristol net. You could only laugh, which was what we did.

Half an hour later Flo made it 3–0. Simpson, on the left, sent another inch-perfect cross to Flo, outside the small square at the far post, and the big Norwegian visibly steadied himself before connecting. It didn't look like a cleanly struck shot, bouncing off the balding turf, but it was well-directed, wide of the keeper, and finished up in the back of the net. Flo was jubilant; so were his team-mates. A striker's league-duck had been comprehensively broken that day with a brace of important goals.

This time there would be no last-minute surrender. Our only real scare came three minutes into extra time, when Torpey got on the end of a centre from Doherty, but his point-blank header was brilliantly tipped over by Mike Stowell.

When the referee blew the final whistle seconds later, I already knew from whispers in the crowd that other results that day had gone our way. Huddersfield had gone down 3–0 at Ipswich; Albion had been massacred 4–0 by The Blues. Only Sheffield had managed to overturn the half-time tables, beating Tranmere 3–2 with a last-gasp, 90th-minute goal. At Oxford, Watford had hung on for a scoreless draw and an away point.

These many scorelines meant that we had got what we wanted. We had 55 points and we were in sixth place, a point clear of Watford and two points clear of the chasing trio, West Brom, Sheffield and

Huddersfield. We had two games in hand of all of these teams except for Sheffield, who had played only a single game more than us.

Back in January, Graham Taylor of Watford had opined that Wolves would do better coming from behind with a late run at promotion. We were no longer behind; we were now in play-off position, in that crucial sixth place. From now on, the task would be to stay there.

33

Aerial Bombardment

I had expected to find in Bury a threadbare remnant of a once-prosperous cotton-mill town – a Grimethorpe of the textile industry, tattered at the edges, with, here and there, an occasional burst of colour to remind itself of palmier days.

The reality, as Len pulled us off the M62 on to the A56, was different. On both sides of the Manchester Road the dark, brick houses looked solid and comfortable in the bright March evening; on the downhill slope the synagogue on the right was quiet, its doors closed.

The stewards at Gigg Lane were friendly, ushering us right on to the parking apron at the front entrance of the ground. It was a kindness much appreciated by Len: he has a gammy leg and, although he never complained, I could tell that the long hikes from some parking lots were troublesome for him.

I said something about the friendliness of the place to Ian Willars when I bumped into him inside. His Grace of the *Evening Mail* was scathing about the Bury ground. It had nothing to offer, Ian told me, not even a cuppa or a programme. I could see his point: an hour and a half before kick-off we could see, in the restaurant to our right, the great and the good sitting to their dinner at tables laid with white cloths but, for hacks and their ilk, there was not so much available as even a mouthful of PG Tips. Even the match programmes – I went back outside to buy a couple for Len and myself – were the originals from the cancelled game, two weeks before. Still, the team sheets were free.

Whatever the Duke's misgivings about Gigg Lane, not a hint of them was evident in his match report the following day; his readers, as always, were presented with a balanced succinct report of events on the pitch.

Those events were not pretty to watch. Bury's sole attacking ploy seemed to be that of aerial bombardment. Time after time high balls were pumped hopefully into Wolves' area; time after time the tactic failed. Mike Stowell's handling was at first unsure but, as the match wore on, he grew in stature and confidence. In the end, he was probably our man of the match.

In the second half, as Bury's strategy became more transparently ineffective, I asked my neighbour, an ardent Bury supporter, why his team persisted with the high ball. His answer was devastatingly simple: 'It's the way the manager forces them to play.'

I had no way of knowing if it was this policy that had dropped Bury into the relegation zone. When they'd come to Molineux back in September, they'd been riding high in fourth place, a couple of points and three places above us; they'd been beaten 1–0 that day and had since gone into freefall. They were, in fact, the only side in the division without an away win.

That night they never looked like having a home win. The trouble was that Wolves didn't look like winning either. Flo had a great chance after eight minutes but, with the goal at his mercy, he hastily shot over the bar. Just before half-time the Norwegian put in a good cross to Robbie but our boy wonder's tame header was easily saved by Dean Kiely. Ten minutes from the end, Neil Emblen, tireless as ever, got forward into a good position but his shot from just inside the area was all power and no direction.

By then, even the Wolves fans were beginning to leave Gigg Lane. Bury were masters of the 0–0 scoreline; from the start, this game had the same result written all over its unpretty face.

The post-match press 'conference' was held in the elegant surroundings of the Bury boot-room. Colin Lee sat on top of a black rubbish bin; the white-washed wall opposite him was covered with pairs of boots and trainers – they looked like beetle-couples trying to climb towards the sanctuary of the ceiling. Or Bury, trying to clamber out of the relegation zone.

Colin didn't share the disappointment that Wolves fans felt with the result. A point had been won, he reminded the scribes clustered around his dustbin, a point that moved Wolves a fraction further away from the chasing pack.

'Six months ago,' Colin said, 'we'd probably have lost a game like that.'

It was an honest reminder of how far we'd come. I don't think any of the journalists would have disagreed with Colin's assessment.

David Instone, of the *Express and Star*, wanted to know how Kevin Muscat's hand was coming along and whether the Australian would be fit for the following Saturday's game, away to Barnsley.

There was every chance he'd play, Colin said. They'd found a special glove to protect the broken bones and Muscat was back in training.

What kind of training, David pressed, did it include physical contact?

'You know what Muzzy is like,' Colin said, trying to keep a straight face, 'he never makes physical contact with anybody.'

'He didn't say that!'

Muscat was laughing as I recounted the gaffer's words to him. Kevin was standing alongside Lee Naylor and Fernando Gomez outside the boot room, all of them in Wolves tracksuits.

'He also told us,' I went on, 'that you've got this miracle glove to protect your hand –'

'I haven't even seen it yet!'

'– and that you'll probably be playing against Barnsley on Saturday.'

'Did he say that?'

'He surely did,' I told him.

The Australian smile broadened. Me, I felt happy just knowing that we'd probably have Muzzy back on Saturday . . .

34

The Numbers Game

It was a numbers game from here on in, we all knew that. The numbers, possibilities and permutations rattled backwards and forwards in the car on the road north for the game against Barnsley. Ged Scott of the *Birmingham Post* was driving; Mike Jones of Beacon Radio was in the back. Neither man is a Wolves fan, but both of them have covered Wanderers in action for so long that they're kindly disposed to the men in old-gold and black.

Wolves were in the driving seat that morning, as far as the last play-off spot was concerned. By failing to win the war of attrition at Bury, we had failed to widen significantly the gap between ourselves and the chasing pack, but we were still at the head of the column. With only ten games remaining, our fate was in our own hands – if we kept on winning, then our pursuers could not overtake us.

The top of the table on that Saturday morning had a comforting look about it:

Place	Team	Games to Play	Points
1.	Sunderland	9	82
2.	Ipswich	9	70
3.	Bradford	10	67
4.	Birmingham	9	67
5.	Bolton	10	64
6.	Wolves	10	56
7.	Watford	9	54
8.	West Brom	9	53
9.	Sheffield	10	53
10.	Huddersfield	9	53
11.	Grimsby	12	50

As the miles slid behind us, we exhausted the possibilities. Grimsby, with games in hand, could overhaul Wolves – but they were going through a lean spell. The same could be said of Watford; Albion also seemed to have run out of steam. Huddersfield were playing Birmingham that day and, even away, you'd have to fancy The Blues – Trevor Francis was already talking about taking the second automatic promotion spot. The danger, we figured, would probably come from Sheffield – three points behind but with a game in hand.

None of which calculations would matter a tinker's belch if Wolves themselves didn't do the business at Oakwell Stadium.

★

Some days stay with you forever. The day of the Barnsley game was one of them. It had everything – echoes of home, heart-stopping excitement, an unbelievable winner in the dying seconds.

Young Seamus Crowe was my reminder of home. Youth team players don't usually travel to away games so I was surprised to see Seamus inside the ground, a couple of hours before kick-off.

Seamus was glowing with youth and health – and pride.

'Colin said I was playing well so I should come along with the seniors in the coach today,' he said.

Had he told his Mam and Dad back in Galway?

'I phoned them,' Seamus said, 'I told them on the phone.'

There was no need to ask if the Crowe family was as proud as punch. Instead I asked if the fellows on the coach had taken the mickey out of the newcomer on board.

'I had to make the coffee for them.' Seamus was laughing. They could have all the coffee in Brazil just as long as he was on that bus.

The road ahead for any young professional footballer is a minefield. Casualties are inevitable. A week earlier, a promising Wolves youngster, Adam Proudlock, had broken his leg in a youth game and would miss at least the rest of the season. Back in the 1960s, injury had put an end to the young career of Ted Farmer, who had been scoring goals at a rate that looked likely to make him a Wolves legend. The game is littered with broken bones and careers destroyed: I mention Ted Farmer because his book, *This Heartbreak Game*, conveys better than any other the agony and the ecstasy of a footballing life. For successful players, the game is a goldmine today, but the odds are stacked against any youngster who dreams of finding his fortune there. I hope Seamus makes the grade.

Colin Lee had a surprise in store for us. For the first time since he had taken over, Colin fielded his side in 3–5–2 formation. Richards, Curle and Emblen lined up in front of Mike Stowell; Muscat, Sedgley, Osborn, Corica and Gilkes were strung across the midfield; Robbie Keane partnered Haavard Flo up front.

It was an attacking formation that had Barnsley under early pressure. A good move saw Robbie link up with Muscat, who passed to Sedgley but his effort was cleared. Only a quarter of an hour had passed and the locals were giving stick to their own side. Barnsley were stung into action. Hignett was on target with a header but Stowell saved comfortably. Deeno, charging out of defence, was fouled in midfield by Dyer: Mr Dean waved his yellow card. Flo, helping out in defence, was dispossessed by Hignett but, fortunately, his powerful grasscutter was just wide from 25 yards.

Not until the 28th minute did Wolves force their first corner. A minute later Flo was readying himself in the box to shoot when Morgan put in a telling tackle. Just two minutes later Craig Hignett, out on the right, swung in a shot-cum-cross which rebounded off the far post and then ricocheted cruelly off the shins of the inrushing Dean Richards to finish up in the back of the net. The Oakwell Stadium went wild.

It went even wilder a couple of minutes later. Following a Corica foul on Moses, Scott Jones struck a free kick from just outside the area; it was a low shot which, to my eye, took a slight deflection before beating Mike Stowell on the left. Two–nil to Barnsley with just over a half-hour gone; it was no wonder the Oakwell erupted. For a misty-eyed moment the south Yorkshire faithful must have been dreaming again of the Premiership.

Yet the scoreline was unfair. I said as much to Ian Willars sitting beside me. His Grace ignored me: he went on puffing furiously at his pipe while he dictated faultless copy into his mobile phone.

We were back in the game four minutes before half-time. Kevin Muscat put in a good cross and who should rise in the box to head home but Neil Emblen . . . ('I don't know what he was doing up there,' Colin Lee would say with a grin after the match, 'but there he was anyway.') It was why Molineux loved him: like Kevin Muscat, Emblen had 'never say die' inscribed on his heart.

Both sides turned the heat up after half-time. Corica, bustling forward, forced a corner, but the result was a free out. A wild back-pass from Curle put Wolves' goal at risk but Stowell booted the ball away for a throw-in. Keith's free kick from inside his own half was headed out by Eaden for a corner. Another corner resulted: Osborn's volley was saved but Emblen buried the rebound in the net. Mr Dean muffled our cheers with an offside whistle. Robbie was through but his half-volley was too high.

The game was threatening to explode as the pressure boiled. Keith was yellow-carded for pulling Dyer. It seemed to me that Barnsley were getting on top. Only a brilliant save by Stowell from Eaden kept us in the game.

Two minutes later, in the 73rd minute, Robbie Keane was replaced by David Connolly. It was a muted departure for our top goalscorer. For over a month past, Robbie had looked tired: this was his sixth game without scoring. Maybe, as Colin had said, Robbie was suffering from vaccinations and inoculations; perhaps he was just worried about going to Nigeria. Whatever the reason for the absence of goals, the Wolfpack applauded him: everybody knew just how much of a loss he would be to our promotion challenge. You could only pray that he would come back again safe and sound.

It was a measure of Wolves' 'Irishness' that one Irish international was replaced by another. David Connolly was barely on the pitch when he challenged Bullock in the Barnsley goal for a bouncing ball and managed to push the ball home past the advancing keeper. Afterwards the Barnsley manager, John Hendrie, would contemptuously dismiss the score as 'an ale-house goal': it was a colourful phrase but mostly you could see the colour of sour grapes on the manager's angry mouth.

The best was still to come. Wolves were fired up now, not content to sit back and take their away point. Time after time they surged forward, hunting for the winner. It came in the last minute of the game. Dean Richards went charging up the right flank as if he had a fire in his shorts and put in a running tackle on a Barnsley defender who was attempting to clear; this time the ball broke favourably and Deeno rode his luck, powering onwards before unleashing an unstoppable shot from just inside the penalty area.

The Wolfpack broke into delirious singing: 3–2 in the last few seconds! Could heaven be an improvement on this? Promotion, perhaps, but not much else; not sex or money or drugs or anything else that man has invented or discovered.

It was epic stuff, this fight-back in Yorkshire. If old Will had lived in this football age he might have saved his Agincourt words for this gob-smacking occasion, when 'gentlemen in England now abed will think themselves accursed they were not there' to see such Molineux heroics crowned by Deeno's screamer . . .

So I get carried away . . . why not? It was the most memorable away day of the season; like the Wolfpack behind the goal on my left, I didn't want the day to end. I understood their reluctance to leave the scene of such a triumph; when, at last, they made their way towards the exits, they were still singing as they went.

Elsewhere that Saturday the results were mixed among the chasing pack. Sheffield had whipped Port Vale 3–0. Huddersfield had managed a 1–1 draw against the Blues. Watford had been the victim of another scoreless draw against Bury. At the Hawthorns the Baggies had gone down 1–0 to Ipswich. What it all meant was that we were still in sixth place, now three points clear of the pack. I had grown to love Yorkshire on my weekly college excursions to Bretton Hall but never had those rounded hills and folded valleys looked so lovely as on that day at Barnsley.

That night, back in Wolverhampton, I searched among a pile of papers until I found an updated Nationwide fixtures list that I had picked up on my travels. At the start of the season I had carefully written into my diary all of Wolves' fixtures, home and away, but now, at last, I dared to enter a few new dates in my diary. They were, of course, the semi-finals and the final of the play-offs . . .

35

War and Wembley

We had no game the following week: the last Saturday in March was set aside for European Championship qualifying games. Our match against

Grimsby was rescheduled for the last week of the season, just a few days before our very last game – a home tie against Bradford.

That Saturday at Wembley, England dispatched Poland comfortably enough, thanks to a hat-trick from Scholes of Manchester United.

It wasn't football that dominated our television screens that weekend. NATO warplanes were in the air over the Balkans, trying to bomb a defiant Serbia into submission; meanwhile the Serb leader, Slobodan Milosevic, unleashed a reign of 'ethnic cleansing' that filled the mountainous roads of Kosovo with terrified refugees and darkened our TV world with the faces of fear and hatred and death.

In such a context of terror, the cancellation of Ireland's game against Macedonia barely registered a blip on the monitors. And yet the loss of the match was a reminder of how far we had failed to travel in this age of progress. My grandfather had shouldered his Connaught Ranger's rifle in that Great War where the generals had sent a generation to its death and ruled football out of order on the rubble of no man's land; now, at the other end of the century, the Balkans were in flames again, the killing was resumed and football was still out of order. From the generations that had gone before us we had learned only how to repeat their mistakes.

I spent that weekend in London. My mate, John, a native of County Cork, lives directly opposite White Hart Lane. When I lifted my eyes from the TV screen in John's sitting-room, I could see the Spurs stadium across the road, wrapped in its own silence. Football players and football managers are not notorious for their high IQ levels, yet even the worst of them could never visit such devastation upon their fellow creatures as could the generals and the politicians; opponents might bite your legs or up-end you lock, stock and smoking barrels – but at least they'd leave you your gold fillings and the fare home.

No – I don't think we should hand over the running of the world to the football community, but it's no harm to remind ourselves that football hooligans are not the worst vermin in the universe.

That Saturday morning, on my way to visit some friends in Maida Vale, I encountered the friendly face of football. On the tube, heading towards Baker Street station, a group of Poles were engaged in animated and puzzled conversation beside me, trying to make sense of the overhead Underground map; in broken English, one of them turned to me for help. They followed me off the train at Baker Street like kids behind a teacher;

they gathered round, at the big map in the station, and exclaimed with glee, pointing out to one another the name of Wembley. They'd flown in just that morning from Chicago; they would return on Sunday and be at work on Monday in the Windy City.

'Is a long way, yes?' their spokesman smiled at me.

It was a long way, I agreed. I'd like to have spent longer with them, to learn what they did, over there in Chicago, but they were anxious to be on their way, and we shook hands and they left me with a litany of thanks, trailing their red scarves behind them. I thought of them later that afternoon, switching channels in John's house between Wembley and the war, and I had not a little sympathy for them. On my Wolves trail I had learned what it was to go home defeated . . . but at least you got to go home.

I headed for the West End that Saturday night, to see *Gross Indecency* at the Gielgud Theatre. Based on court transcripts and other contemporary documents, the play tells the tragic story of the three trials of Oscar Wilde. Poor Oscar's genius could not save him from a hypocritical Victorian London that was no less puritanical than the priest-ridden Irish society he had left: the tale of his incarceration in Reading Gaol and his early death from a broken heart needs no re-telling here.

I couldn't help thinking about the contrast with the fate of Graham Rix, the Chelsea coach. On the previous day Rix had been sentenced to 12 months' imprisonment for having sex with an underage girl in a London hotel. Oscar had been pauperised by his conviction for homosexuality, his name immediately removed from his hugely successful West End plays; Chelsea FC had announced that Rix, convicted of underage sex, would find his well-paid job waiting for him on his release.

There was another irony. England had triumphed that day at Wembley under new manager, Kevin Keegan; the FA had sacked his predecessor, Glenn Hoddle, because he believed in a female faith healer and had made injudicious remarks about reincarnation. It just makes you wonder.

On Tuesday morning I travelled back up from Euston to Wolverhampton, in good time for the evening game against Crewe.

Over 24,000 turned up at Molineux to see Wolves demolish the Railwaymen 3–0. Crewe lost Chris Lightfoot, as early as the 13th minute, for a second bookable offence on Connolly, and from that moment on the outcome was inevitable. Robinson scored a minute later; Flo made it 2–0 about ten minutes afterwards, and Muscat wrapped up a comfortable victory from the penalty spot 11 minutes from the final whistle.

Molineux rocked as if the good times were already rolling in. Sheffield had been surprisingly beaten 2–1 by Oxford in one of the few games played over the weekend, which meant that Wolves, still in sixth place, had drawn six points clear of their pursuers.

For the first time at a post-match conference, Colin Lee was asked serious questions about Wolves' promotion chances. Like the rest of us, Colin knew that Wolves could miss out on the play-offs only if they themselves threw away the chance. As always, however, Colin was down-to-earth; perhaps, like the Wolfpack, he remembered those other occasions when Wolves, in sight of the winning post, had run out of puff.

He repeated yet again that you had to take each game by itself. 'Ask me in a week's time,' he said. 'We have two critical matches coming up over the Easter weekend – talk to me after that.'

36

In the Wolf's Lair

Well, in John Richards's office, anyway. When you've grown used to the wide, open spaces of Molineux and the bright airiness of its stands and tunnels, it feels almost claustrophobic in the narrow corridor leading to John's office. Jenny of the cut-glass vowels led the way around the corners of the corridor until we came to the door with John's name and title printed on the polished brass plate.

The managing director of Wolverhampton Wanderers FC was expecting me on that morning of 1 April. Back in December, on Boxing Day in sodden Swindon, I'd introduced myself to John, explaining about my book assignment and wondering whether I could see him sometime. Over three months and a couple of phone calls later, here I was in the office of the Wolves boss, shaking his hand and being asked if I was enjoying my year.

I told him, truthfully, that I was having one of the best years of my life. I could have enlarged on that, easily and cheerfully, but I was there for the chance to listen to John Richards, not the other way around.

For the next hour I did just that – listen to John Richards talking fluently and happily about his life and times with Wolves. I made no tape-recording of our words; neither did I make any notes there and then, although I did, immediately afterwards, make a few basic jottings of what John had said. Instead I listened carefully, allowing myself to be absorbed by his words, trying to form an impression of the man who was the hands-on supremo of the club I loved.

In his account of his growing-up I heard uncanny echoes of my own youth. John Richards was brought up in Warrington, in what was then Lancashire but has since become part of Cheshire. He was the eldest of five boys in a working-class family; his father worked in a local steelworks. He was a bright boy. He was diligent too, working hard to secure his place at grammar school. After O-levels, he had to decide between having to go to work or staying on at school to take his A-levels.

'It was a time when most fellows left school to bring in an extra wage at home,' John said, 'but my mother wanted me to continue with my education. She encouraged me – she always did.'

Two years later, teenager Richards had his A-levels in his pocket together with a place at teacher training college. That was when Wolves entered the picture, uttering promises of a different kind of future for the youngster who had made a name for himself in school football. Mother once more offered her encouragement: Richards signed for Wolves as a professional on a wage of £25 a week.

'I was 18,' he said to me, 'and I was earning almost as much as my Dad was taking home.'

I have a hunch that the world of education lost a good teacher when John Richards opted for football. He still has about him something of the air of an old-fashioned headmaster. When you see him around Molineux he is always immaculately turned out in collar and tie and, usually but not always, a crested blazer. He always listens to you attentively and he is unfailingly polite. I reminded him of how I'd seen him in a service area off the M1, north of London, surrounded by a bunch of fans when we were *en route* to play Palace the previous October.

'You have to do that kind of thing,' John said. 'You have to listen to what the fans are saying.'

We'd been doing badly back then; Mark McGhee had made his exit a week later. I wanted to know if John's motorway listening exercise had had anything to do with the change of manager.

'Everything had to be taken into account,' John said, avoiding my question with as much skill as he'd once avoided tackles in his goal-scoring days.

The memory of how those days ended at Molineux is still, I think, a source of hurt to John Richards. Unable to command a regular first team place with Wolves in the 1982–83 season, he was on loan at Derby County when manager Graham Hawkins recalled him to Molineux. It was a time which is remembered without warmth in Wolverhampton: the Bhatti brothers owned the shop; Derek Dougan was the hands-on boss. Richards still didn't get regular first-team football, making only two appearances for Wolves, who were then in the old Second Division. What grieves him about his move to Maritimo of Madeira is that, leaving as he did in August 1983, he had no opportunity to say goodbye to the fans he loved – and who loved him. Sir Jack Hayward brought him on to the Molineux Board after the death of the legendary Billy Wright; his appointment as managing director came in 1997.

He's a contented man, is John Richards. He has what he calls 'the best job in the world'.

'And you can't get fired,' I said, 'like the manager.'

He laughed. 'The Board can get me out too,' he said.

This educated, understated, modest man is well suited to his job. He never had any hankering, he told me, to be a traditional football manager. 'I never knew about team tactics . . . I was never interested in that side of it. Some guys have it – you can see it in guys like Kenny Hibbitt and Keith Curle.'

'At half-time in a game, if things are going badly,' John went on, 'I couldn't tell you how to change the game for the better.'

'You must be the only guy in Molineux who couldn't,' I said, thinking of the half-time pronouncements overheard in the press room and in the tunnels.

'I have enough problems of a different kind,' John said.

'And if we make it into the Premiership,' I said, 'we're going to have even more problems.'

'Ah,' said John, smiling, 'but wouldn't it be nice to have them!'

But if we made it, I pressed, would out-of-contract players such as

Dean Richards be given new contracts to keep them at the club?

'That depends on Deeno's demands,' John said. 'Maybe there's another Bosnian player out there who's just a good as Deeno but whose demands are a lot less.'

Sir Jack, I figure, has found in JR a safe pair of hands for his investment. John Richards, it seems to me, knows what a pound will buy but, more importantly, he knows the enduring value of human qualities such as loyalty and commitment.

When Jenny knocked and entered quietly to ask if John would soon be free to take an important phone call, I doubted very much that any such call was about to come in. I didn't mind: it was a polite and acceptable way to remind John that he had other items on his agenda that morning besides socialising with a scribe from the west of Ireland.

Galway seemed both far and near when I stepped out into the morning sunshine and stood for a moment beside the statue of William Ambrose. Far, because I had never dreamed, back in Galway the year before, that I would so soon be privileged to sit and talk with the boss of Molineux; near, because John Richards's own words of Warrington youth and a loving mother had so poignantly reminded me of my own young years in Galway.

I drove straight from Molineux to Newbridge. Walking across the vast training ground, I could hear the thud of boot on ball and the urgent cries of the players at the far end. Neil Emblen gave me a wave as I approached.

'How're things?' I asked.

He beamed. 'There's a great spirit in the camp.'

How well he put it. The Wolves players were giddy as schoolboys let loose in the Place Pigalle. If you could bottle the optimism that was bubbling all over Newbridge that sunny morning, you'd put the makers of Viagra out of business.

John Ward put all of them through some complicated ball-control and dribbling exercises, with an edge of competitiveness added by dividing the bunch into three competing groups. Mockery and mickey-taking were an integral ingredient but they encouraged one another always, like youngsters hungry for the teacher's gold star.

Afterwards John took the whistle for a series of urgent, seven-a-side games. Each game lasted for four minutes; even the 'resting' team was involved, as sideline providers to the participants. The matches were short, sharp and fiercely competitive. David Connolly netted a glancing header and swung round with upraised arms as if he had scored the winner at the Hawthorns. When Haavard Flo thumped in a powerful shot from 20 yards, I'm sure they heard his grunt of satisfaction on the mountain tops of Norway.

Colin Lee was patrolling the sideline with the intensity of Fagin putting a value on his gemstones.

He didn't look as if he'd want his valuations interrupted, but I chanced it anyway.

'There's a fantastic atmosphere here this morning, Colin.' That's me, always ready with the searching question.

'And we have to keep it rolling now,' Colin said.

'You will,' I said, 'you will.'

I don't know if he heard me. He was off again, patrolling, evaluating, plotting a passage through Easter and beyond . . .

37

Easter 1999

For the first of Colin Lee's two 'crucial' games, Portsmouth came to Molineux on Easter Saturday. They came burdened by difficulties on and off the pitch – financial problems which had the club in administration; poor performances which had the team hovering dangerously close to the relegation zone.

When Pompey set out on the long journey back to the south coast that evening, manager Alan Ball's kitbag of woes weighed even heavier. Wolves didn't score until the 72nd minute – another mighty Muscat strike from some 25 yards out – but they seemed to me to be in control for most of the game. They were frustrated, too, by a packed midfield:

Alan Ball's admitted policy was that he had come to Molineux 'to frustrate – to spoil the game'.

Ball claimed that the sending-off of Jeff Peron for a second bookable offence, a quarter of an hour before Muscat's goal, had been the turning point of the game. I took Colin Lee's view of the matter – I would, wouldn't I? – that Wolves would have won anyway.

Three minutes after Muscat's goal came the game's most bizarre incident. Awford's awful(!) long back-pass from the halfway line was 'dummied' by one of his team-mates, allowing the ball to run on to the keeper; David Connolly, meanwhile, was chasing from the centre circle on a hunt-and-harry mission that probably intimidated keeper Knight into handling the back-pass just inside his own area. Wolves dealt out summary punishment for the error. Simon Osborn's indirect free kick was touched to Flo who thumped an unstoppable ball low into the Pompey net. It was a well-worked set piece, one I'd watched more than once on the Newbridge training ground.

Molineux's festive mood was heightened by the public announcer's recitation of the rest of the day's results. Sheffield had lost further ground, going down 2–1 at Barnsley. The inevitable cheer greeted the news that our well-beloved neighbours from The Hawthorns had been beaten 3–0 by Sunderland. Bolton had been held to a scoreless draw at Oxford. Watford alone had kept pace with us, managing a late goal to defeat Tranmere 2–1. Our announcer was ecstatic. 'We're in sixth place he boomed, 'and we're seven points clear of Watford!'

Alan Ball was less than ecstatic. At the post-match press conference he vented his anger on a young reporter who ventured to ask him if he felt that Pompey could still manage to avoid relegation.

Ball's expression was grim as he rounded on the unfortunate hack. 'We don't need our local people,' he spat, 'starting to get a panic going – we need a little bit of local support, not like the front page story you had yesterday!'

After the unhappy Ball had left, I had a word with the journalist. Mark Storey writes for the *Portsmouth Evening News*; the previous day the newspaper had run a front page story on the club's administration crisis.

'But you didn't write that piece?' I asked Mark.

'Tell that to Alan Ball,' he grinned.

The episode highlighted the fragile relationship between any local reporter and the club he covers. David Instone, for instance, spends his working life writing about Wolves; inevitably he builds up close relationships with many of the players and the management team. Yet he is not a mouthpiece for the club; any reporter worth his salt has to retain the right to criticise what he sees as inadequacies or failings.

Players and managers are not made of stone; with Shylock they can say, 'If you prick us, do we not bleed?' They carry our dreams on their backs but that doesn't mean they should have to bear the cross of personal or offensive criticism. The line between legitimate and unfair criticism is always a fine one; for a local reporter, working day in, day out with his home team, that line is a fence of barbed wire. Ask Alan Ball, he'll explain it to you. But don't mention the 'R' word . . .

★

The press box at Bramall Lane is spacious and airy. There are plenty of power points for the journalists to plug in their phones and laptops, with elbow room enough to finger your keyboard or scribble your notes.

Trouble is, the area is shielded from the outside world by thick sheets of plate glass. You have a splendid view of the action on the pitch but you can't hear boot connect with ball or hear Mike Stowell roaring to his backs 'Keeper!' as he surges forward to collect a high cross. Even the roar of the Easter Monday crowd was muted, like an explosion distantly heard.

I said as much to David Instone at half-time.

He looked at me over the rim of the teacup.

'Go up to the television gantry, Kevin,' he said. 'Loads of room up there.'

What David called the gantry was a long, open area under the roof of the main stand. The Wolves and Sheffield players were already on the pitch for the re-start when I was making my way past the earphoned-heads of the row of radio commentators. At the far end of the area I could see the TV camera operator getting ready for action.

The gantry was no isolation ward. Here you were exposed to the day and the game. The noise roared up at us like thunder exploding skywards. A waist-high iron rail separated us from freefall; should you stumble, the 20-inch net of rusting netwire looked like it might arrest your downward flight for a second or two. I found an empty bar stool and drew myself close to the rail. It was still 0–0: everything still to play for and I was in the perfect place to feel it all.

As the second half was kicked off, what I felt most in my eagle's eyrie was the intensity of the Bramall Lane crowd, urging their team on. The Blades were not having a good Easter. The previous Saturday they'd gone down 2–1 in a south Yorkshire derby against Barnsley; that defeat had been all the harder to swallow as Barnsley's winning goal had come in the 90th minute. On the same day, Watford had won, thus leap-frogging over Sheffield into seventh place. To get back into play-off contention, Sheffield needed a win: the players knew it – and how the crowd knew it! Wave upon wave of noise swelled around the ground as Sheffield searched for an opening.

Their goal came in the 17th minute of the second half. Morris sent a rapier-like cross into the Wolves box and Marcelo barely touched the ball to glance it past Stowell. Bramall Lane exploded with delirium; the ground rocked to the chanting of 'United! United!' Beside me the radio commentators told the story of the goal in excited, breathless tones. Sheffield manager, Steve Bruce, was on his feet, urging his players to steady the ship towards home.

Behind the goal to my left the travelling Wolfpack refused to be silenced. Wolves had shown their teeth – and their courage – with fighting late goals at Loftus Road and at Barnsley: we knew that all was not lost. Maybe it was Barnsley Colin Lee was thinking of when he pushed Neil Emblen up front, alongside Flo and Connolly – the ploy had worked once in Yorkshire, why shouldn't it work again?

Lee's next move, with eight minutes remaining, was to replace Connolly with Steve Corica. The Australian was no more than two minutes on the field when he bustled into the Sheffield area and, goalward bound, was knocked over by a Sheffield defender. The referee was deaf to the righteous cries of the Wolfpack for a penalty; a free kick from just outside the area was his uncharitable verdict.

It seemed to take ages for the kick to be taken. Simon Osborn waited beside the ball while Sheffield built, demolished and then rebuilt their wall. A couple of Wolves players pushed in and out of the wall; the ref. wanted it further back.

Finally he blew, and we watched, enchanted, as Osborn's kick curved and looped above the wall and the top corner of the net shook and the ground rocked again, but now it was the roar of the Wolfpack that shook the stanchions of Bramall Lane.

Five minutes of reverberating excitement remained. Those minutes belonged, mostly, to Wolves. Sheffield's Kozluk was sent off for a second bookable offence; Steve Bruce made two late substitutions. At the end it was Corica again, belting the ball too high from a great cross-field pass by Neil Emblen.

It ended in a 1–1 draw, but it was the Wolves fans who cheered at the final whistle; the locals, robbed so late of their victory, contented themselves with booing the referee. I knew how they felt; I knew too well the numbness of losing in the closing minutes of a game.

Wolves, on the other hand, seemed to have forgotten how to lose: since the Swindon deluge, we had lost only once – and that to a scrambled goal against Sunderland. As Neil Emblen had said to me on the training ground a few days before, morale was high in the camp. Neil and his team-mates waved and clapped to the Wolfpack at the end and were deservedly applauded in return. Yet the loudest, warmest applause from the Wolves end was for Colin Lee and John Ward. Wolves had steel in their soul now and self-belief in their bones; we all knew that these strengths had not suddenly bloomed at Molineux like accidental flowers on the roadside.

38

An Encounter with the Gaffer

A couple of mornings later the strangest thing happened on the Newbridge training ground.

I made my usual leisurely way around the perimeter to stand on the far side of proceedings, where the breeze came at your back. The first team squad was obviously still on a well-earned break, after playing three games in seven days; Keith Curle was taking charge of a training session with the reserves.

Seamus Crowe waved at me. Dominick Foley shouted hello. (Dominick was back from a loan spell with Greek club Atheneikos, a spell which had ended abruptly with his recall by Wolves as the Greeks had the peculiar notion that they could hold on to Dominick without paying for his services. Dominick was bitter about his experience. He'd enjoyed Athens but now, he said, 'I hope they're relegated because of the way they treated me.')

It was a powerful reserve squad on the pitch that morning. Steve Bull was there, still doggedly striving for fitness; Paul Simpson and Mark Atkins were there; so too were Steve Corica, Fernando Gomez, Adrian Williams, Ryan Green and Robert Niestroj.

John Ward and I exchanged salutations about the precious point at Sheffield and the loveliness of the morning; John moved off after a little while to watch from behind a goal. He's a great believer in knocking balls into the far post – 'It's a goal-scoring area,' he'd enthused to me on an earlier morning. I was content, both with the game in progress and with the bright spring day. Colin Lee was on the opposite touchline, chatting with one of the physios.

When I looked across a few minutes later I was surprised to notice that Colin was making his way around the back of the goal on my right and heading in my direction.

For a second it crossed my mind that perhaps he was going to ask me to move along.

Although neither Colin Lee nor John Ward had ever intimated to me that I was unwelcome, I never took my presence at their training manoeuvres for granted. I'd say good morning to them, speak when I was spoken to and stand aside to let them get on with their work. And for them and the players it *was* work; I was always conscious of that. I'd fetch an errant ball now and again for Mike Stowell or one of the other players but generally I never attempted to speak to anybody while work was in progress. Sometimes I'd look up at the blue Black Country sky and I'd shake my head in bafflement at the miracle that had brought me here from Galway.

When Colin came and stood beside me, I knew he wasn't there to ask me to leave. Maybe he'd just learned to accept my sideline presence; maybe he too considered me, as one of the journalists had laughingly put it, 'a fan with a pen'. Whatever the reason, Colin Lee was in a humour to talk.

Mostly he talked about himself. For 10 or 15 minutes I listened with a kind of awe to the Wolves gaffer talking about his boyhood and the road that had led him to Molineux.

He had grown up in Torquay, on the south-west coast. It's more rugby than soccer country; Colin's own father had been an accomplished rugby player. Colin himself was a superior athlete: by the time he was 15 he was playing for the Devon county side in both football and rugby.

'You were a three-quarter,' I said, measuring his height and lean strength.

'No, I was a scrum-half.' He grinned, seeing the question in my expression. 'I wasn't so big then.'

Professional sport was how he wanted to earn his living: it was going to be either rugby league or pro football.

'My family and I talked it over. I loved rugby but for league I'd have had to go north and it was a long way in those days without motorways.'

It was odd: just the week before, John Richards had been telling me how the bounce of a ball had diverted him from teaching to football – now here was Colin Lee explaining how a similar metaphorical bounce had led to another career diversion. The world of rugby league can only speculate on what the youngster from Torquay might have achieved with the oval ball.

Colin Lee's road led first to Bristol City. His wise parents, however, encouraged him to pursue a parallel option – just in case.

'I did a chef's course; a proper two years' training, and I finished it.'

There was no need to tell me that he'd finished it: I knew little about Lee but I knew enough to know that.

Although he still cooks occasionally at home, the chef's career proved unnecessary. Colin Lee had a successful career, including spells at Chelsea and Spurs, before moving into management and, eventually, into the Molineux hot seat.

It was his performance there that intrigued me. The current Wolves team, apart from Haavard Flo, was drawn from precisely the same squad of players that Colin Lee had inherited from his predecessor, yet they had been transformed from a bunch of inconsistent no-hopers into a bonded unit in pursuit of promotion: even while Colin and I were talking, the reserves were battling in a practice game as if it were a Wembley cup final.

'I know you say at press conferences that it's all a team effort at Molineux,' I pressed, 'but you must be doing something different with the team. Is it something instinctive – or something else?'

'Everybody knows their job now,' Colin said. 'Like our set pieces. We practise them every Thursday and Friday. They all know where they have to be. They all know what the variations are. Other clubs are watching us: they study our moves, so we have to be able to change them.

'It's the same with the back eight. Whether we're playing 4–4–2 or 3–5–2, the defence has to play as an eight-man unit when we're being attacked. We practise all the time so that everybody knows where they're supposed to be in that eight-man defence.'

He broke off to bark advice at one of the players: 'Close up on him! Close up on him when he's going for it like that!'

When he stepped back beside me, he continued as if he'd never interrupted himself: 'Every player gets a typed itinerary every few days so they all know exactly what they'll be doing and when they'll be doing it. They know when they'll be training, they know what time the coach will be leaving, they even know what time they'll be eating.'

I asked him if it was normal practice at big clubs for players to be given such a prepared timetable.

'I don't know,' Colin shrugged. 'It's just the way I like things to be. I like everything to be properly organised.'

The following night, 8 April, I went to Hednesford Town to see the Wolves reserve side play in the semi-final of the Birmingham Senior Cup. Steve Bull was playing in the side; it was his third match outing on the come-back trail. I'd seen the first two; I didn't want to miss any of them.

A lot of other fans felt the same way; the main stand was packed for the 7.45 p.m. kick-off. There was an air of expectancy about the compact Hednesford arena. With Robbie Keane still absent on the unfortunate Nigerian business, we all hungered more than ever for the return of a fully fit Bully.

Inside two minutes he had made his presence felt, his glancing header finding Mark Jones who slotted home. Jones scored again before half-time and completed his hat-trick after eight minutes of the second half. The goal we all wanted to see, however, came 25 minutes into the second half. A lovely through ball from Fernando fell to Bully and our hero forced his way past the Hednesford defence to fire home Wolves' fourth goal. Tescott made it a 5–0 victory for Wolves but the real result of the night was that Bully's wounded knee had stood up to the rigours of the fray. There was relief as well as exultation in the lengthy applause that marked his departure from the pitch a quarter of an hour from the end: Steve was well and truly on the road back.

My own road back from Hednesford was no more than a half-hour drive through Cannock and then straight on to Wolverhampton. My long-serving Kadett was back in Galway; months earlier I had bought a second-hand Corolla from David Sheen, manager of a big car sales outfit in Sutton Coldfield – David is naturally a lunatic Wolves supporter which is obvious proof of the soundness of the many cars he sells. Now, with another good result to keep me company, I was looking forward to the leisurely drive back. With my unerring sense of direction, of course, I found myself heading north on the M6, going precisely the wrong way. What could I do but laugh at myself? Next time, I figured, I'd get Colin Lee to make out my itinerary.

39

Too Close for Comfort

You know the old crack about *Waiting for Godot*: it's the play in which nothing happens twice. Wolves' home game against Crystal Palace was like that, except that it happened more than twice.

Over 23,600 turned up to see it not happen. Hopes were higher than usual at Molineux. Wolves were in fifth place, a point ahead of Bolton, five ahead of Watford. Bolton had a game in hand, but they'd lost their last three games, and so they seemed a comfortable buffer between us and Graham Taylor's team. Colin Lee's organisational medicine was doing the trick: Wolves were having their best end-of-season run for many years.

It was unfortunate that Steve Coppell, the Palace manager, refused to play ball with our dreams. He had his own, it seemed. Coppell had taken over a Palace side in administration and in freefall towards demolition; now they were in the top ten and undefeated in their previous nine games.

They left Molineux with a tenth non-defeat in their team kitbag. Wolves had a few chances but failed to take them. In terms of possession they won the match hands down but the scoreline remained resolutely 0–0. It was the most forgettable game of my season at Molineux.

At half-time, in the press room, I watched Bobbyjo win the Grand National at odds of 10:1. It was an Irish victory but I hadn't a bean on the Carberrys' horse. I had my couple of quid each way on General Wolf – what else would you expect? He ran well but tired near the end and finished well out of the frame. It was not, I hoped, a portent of things to come.

The most important result from the rest of the day's programme came from Vicarage Road, where Watford had beaten Bolton 2–0. The effect of our draw and Watford's win was to leave us in fifth place, now two points ahead of Bolton. Their game in hand still niggled; equally worrying was Watford's closing of the gap. They had won their last three games and were now only three points behind us.

It was almost six o'clock when I left the stadium that evening. The day had turned cold; a chilly wind swept along Waterloo Road. Molineux had about it that dejected look of the morning after, when the party's over and the empty bottles and sticky glasses lie tumbled on the staircase. A few die-hards were huddled around the main entrance, pens and autograph books at the ready. William Ambrose had his back to the stadium, frozen eternally in mid-stride, forever going forward to play the game of his life. I tipped him a salute as I eased the car out and turned towards home: now, more than ever, we needed the steadying hand of William Ambrose Wright to guide us through the dangerous reefs that lay ahead.

The following Tuesday night I went to The Hawthorns. Albion were due at Molineux two weekends later and I wanted to see for myself what kind of threat they posed to our ambitions.

Or so I told myself. I think the truth was that I just wanted to see another football game. It gets into your head, like heroin into a junkie's veins.

Or maybe I just wanted to see the Baggies extend a sweet sequence of five defeats to a round half-dozen. Perish the thought.

Even allowing for my minimal prejudice, I saw little that night to frighten Wolves about the upcoming derby game at Molineux. Swindon had a hatful of chances but seemed determined to squander them. The game ended 1–1.

Albion's manager, Denis Smith, was defensive after the game. Most of Albion's recent difficulties, he seemed to be saying, stemmed from an unfairly critical press. I waited until I had heard Swindon manager Jimmy Quinn's more satisfied words before I left the ground. Winter had returned to the Black Country: frost and ice rimed the few remaining cars in the darkened parking lot.

From elsewhere, too, the news that night was frosty. Bolton had at last arrested their downhill slide by beating Bristol; their home win vaulted them into fifth place, a single point ahead of Wolves. We were still in the last play-off position but Watford's chasing breath seemed too close and too chilly on our nervous necks.

40

A Rearguard Action

My friends at New Cross Hospital's Radio Wulfrun were aggrieved: the powers-that-be at St Andrew's would allow them only one seat in the press box for Wolves' game against Birmingham.

Didn't they know, Ray demanded, that they literally had listeners dying to hear a commentary on Wolves' activities?

His indignation fell on deaf ears. Len would have to cover the game alone. The New Cross patients would have to make do with occasional phoned 'inserts' from St Andrew's to keep them abreast of the day's action.

Len drove: down the M6, on to the Aston Expressway and then left towards the home of the Blues. Birmingham's roads are beyond me. I have mastered London's roads, I have survived Dublin's – but the Second City's roads remain a mystery to me. By way of compensation, I tried to blarney our way into one of the official car-parks, but they weren't having any of that either at St Andrew's.

We were early. We sat upstairs in the small press room and chatted with Bill Hatton of *The Wolf* about our play-off chances. *The Wolf* was taking the Colin Lee line – one game at a time. Their caution was understandable: this was a road they'd travelled too many times before. Like Wolves fans everywhere, they knew what it was to have a long journey end only in tears. With only five games remaining, we were in fifth place but all of us were conscious of the flimsiness of the ice beneath our feet.

I went looking for a bag of chips in the bowels of the Old Stand. The tunnels are cavernous; you'd half-expect the Man in the Iron Mask to stumble, groaning for justice, round one of the echoing corners. He wouldn't want to be looking for a bag of chips . . .

They had none either at the van on the bridge outside the ground. Frankfurters and burgers aplenty but not a chip to be had.

Chip-less, I was on my way back inside when I bumped into the Duke. He listened in astonishment to my heart-wrenching tale of the missing chips.

'Never mind your chips,' His Grace said. 'What you need is a drink.'

As always, the Duke was correct. Two medicinal Scotches warmed my belly and banished all yearning for fried spuds. Maybe I needed them anyway to steel my nerves against my surroundings. The bar was wedged tight with home supporters; there wasn't an old-gold shirt or scarf in sight. I felt like one of the dressed-up RAF escapers from Colditz keeping his mouth shut in a bus packed with Fritzes in Dusseldorf.

Ian moved among them with ducal ease. Greetings were dispensed, hands shaken. Molineux was his beat but he was, after all, a long-serving staffer on Birmingham's own evening paper.

'So,' I said, when we had negotiated a little elbow space. 'Have you spoken to Robbie yet?'

Ireland had, pleasingly, been knocked out of the caper in Nigeria: Robbie Keane would be back with us earlier than we'd dared to hope. But not today.

Ian shook his head. 'I've been ringing everywhere – I've tried his mobile dozens of times – I just couldn't raise him.'

'And his weekly piece in the *Mail*,' I went on. 'Has he written it this week?'

'Of course he has,' Ian said, laughing.

Ian transforms a few words of chat with our Robbie into a ghosted weekly column by the Wolves striker. For Ian it's just another part of a sports journalist's job; for Robbie it's probably handy pin-money, enough to pay for an occasional take-away.

'You couldn't get Robbie,' I said, 'but he has written his piece for you.'

Ian laughed.

'I suppose,' I said, sipping at my Scotch-and-ginger, 'Robbie has told his readers that it was hot and sticky in Nigeria but he's glad he's back now to help Wolves with their promotion run-in?'

'You've read it!' the Duke said.

We both knew otherwise. Newspapers have inches to be filled. Footballers have names to lend to columns.

They're not all done like that. I'm sure Niall Quinn did his own joined-up writing that season for *The Guardian*. And some 20 years ago a Wolves goal-scoring legend also personally wrote and delivered his own column for Wolverhampton's *Express and Star*. I know, because John Richards told me so – with understandable pride.

We had no John Richards that day at St Andrews. We did, however, have Steve Corica. Thirteen minutes after the kick-off, the little Australian took the ball forward, pushed it wide to Emblen and drove on into the box to take the return from Neil; I watched him steady himself before directing the ball low and right into the Blues net.

The Wolfpack behind the goal on my right was ecstatic. I sat on my hands: I was in the middle of the Blues. Across the silenced heads of the locals I caught the eye of Lorraine Hennessy, Wolves' PR officer, and we risked a half-grin.

I was pleased for Corica. Colin had persevered with the Australian, sometimes to the puzzlement – even anger – of the Molineux crowd. More than once I'd heard Corica take stick from the stands: he's an elegant, even dainty, player – and sometimes his apparent reluctance to get 'stuck in' was not well received by a crowd used to the Aussie aggressiveness of Muscat. For myself, I find it impossible to call for the head (or the boots) of a player once I've met him. Which is how it was with Steve Corica. Just once, as the players were leaving the training ground at Newbridge, I'd fallen into step beside him and introduced myself to him. He'd listened attentively and offered me a courteous hand; thereafter he spoke of his upbringing in Melbourne and his liking for Wolverhampton with clarity and affection.

And thereafter, warmed by the memory of a brief encounter with a gracious young man, I wanted Steve Corica to do well.

Now here he was doing just that, putting Wolves ahead in a local derby which was crucial to both teams' progress towards the play-offs. Corica was playing just behind Haavard Flo, in a 4–4–1–1 formation. Our Robbie had left Nigeria but, as the Duke had pointed out, the Irish eagle still hadn't landed. Steve Bull was listed in a Wolves team sheet for the first time since early October but he sat on the bench, his match fitness still in question.

Corica's was the only goal of the game. Wave upon blue wave rolled forward, urged on by a fanatical St Andrew's, but the Wolves defence held firm. Early season leaks in our defence had been well and truly plugged: Wolves had kept a clean sheet in no less than six out of their previous eight games. The result at St Andrew's would make it seven out of nine. Mike Stowell would remember it as the day he broke Bert Williams' goal-keeping record with his 421st appearance in a Wolves jersey.

I found St Andrew's a hostile, intimidating theatre – more so than the Reebok or the Stadium of Light. Maybe it was that I was sitting amid the alien corn; whatever it was, the fingers on my left hand were almost paralysed at the end, frozen into their crossed-for-luck position. Time crawled: again and again I checked my watch to find that far too many minutes remained for comfort.

The home crowd sang 'Singing the Blues'.

And the Wolfpack sang 'We've got the Blues on the run.'

With five minutes to go, Colin Lee called Flo off, to be replaced by Steve Bull. The Wolfpack was delirious: the messiah had returned to his people. 'BUL-LY!' they chanted, 'BUL-LY!'

The other crowd sang: 'Bull-shit! Bull-shit!'

Oh dear. Oscar would have been less than enchanted with such a show of wit. Or whatever it was.

For Trevor Francis, our victory must have been a beaker of gall: Wolves had completed a handsome double over his side. Yet he offered us no sour grapes at the post-match press conference: automatic promotion was now beyond the reach of the Blues but a place in the play-offs seemed a certainty.

Some of the journalists had asked for Steve Corica to come to the press room. In all that long season on the road with Wolves I can only recall one other player being quizzed in the press room by the general body of writers – and that was Steve Bull on the night of his comeback with the reserves against Bolton at Molineux. The more common practice was for a journalist to have a quiet private word with a player before the teams left the ground.

In his suit and tie Corica looked like a well-turned-out schoolboy amid the scrum of scribes. I was standing close to him. When I tapped him on the shoulder and said 'Well done', he turned and smiled his thanks. The scribes wanted answers – but I wanted to touch the man who had scored our winner. Steve looked vulnerable, even fragile, but he gave his answers with aplomb. He was from Melbourne. He was 26. Yes, it was his first goal of the season . . .

It was worth waiting for, I thought. Colin Lee and John Ward probably thought the same. After the final whistle, after hugging their players, the pair of them had trotted over to the Wolfpack, raised hands joined together in triumph, to acclaim and be acclaimed. The cameramen caught the moment: local papers ran the photograph of the triumphant managerial duo, holding hands, beaming at the crowd.

The following week, in 'his' column in the Express and Star, Mike Stowell let us know what the Molineux dressing-room thought of such a carry-on: the photo in question was taped to the wall of the dressing-room under the fresh caption 'WHO SAID ROMANCE WAS DEAD?'

Oscar would have liked that one.

41

A Meeting in the Skies

The day after the Blues game I flew from Birmingham to Dublin. There were chores aplenty in Galway that could wait no longer; I also wanted to see my children. Sara and Georgia met me at Dublin Airport. Lunch was a chatty affair: my own good spirits after the St Andrews result were matched by my daughters', both of them nearing the end of educational courses and excited about the prospects of full-time work.

I knew how they felt. Pushing the little hire car west towards Galway after I'd dropped my daughters off in the city, I had time to reflect on the year gone by. I could hardly believe that the season was almost spent. Only four games remained; beyond that, for the team, lay the possibility of the play-offs and the dream of promotion.

For myself, I no longer knew what lay beyond that football season. When I'd left Galway the previous July, heading slowly east through blinding rain, my way ahead had seemed clear. I would spend the season in Wolverhampton, complete my book commission on the team I had dreamed of since boyhood, and then I would go back to my life in the west of Ireland.

Now the way ahead was less clear, less certain. I had lived my dream for almost a full season now; what I had not anticipated was the way in which I myself would be changed by living out that dream. Whatever dream-like notions I had harboured of following a team which had assumed in my heart almost myth-like status had given way to the reality of motorway miles, sour defeats and hard-won draws. Even my nodding acquaintance with some of the players had divested them of their mythological armour and brought into focus their essentially limited humanity.

Yet even the reality I lived in was edged with the burnished sheen of dreams. The motorways could feel boringly endless and the service area cafés numbingly similar – yet, in my boy's mind, those journeys were still transformed into pilgrimages; each plastic caff became a way-station *en route* to yet another holy shrine and an ancient liturgy.

It was my life in Galway that seemed alien now. I slipped back into it, however, without any great difficulty, working my way through the tasks I had set myself for the week back in Ireland. I'd look up from my desk in my house on the hill on the edge of Galway and through the back window I'd look out over the roofs of the city, over the towers of the university and the green dome of the cathedral, and across the still waters of the bay I'd see the rounded softness of the Clare hills, but in my mind I'd be seeing the flat stretch of Newbridge grass, the players going through their movements as though in balletic slow motion and across the miles I'd hear Colin's voice looming out his conviction that, 'We defend as an eight – that's what makes us hard to beat!'

My mother would have reminded me with a shake of her head that we're never satisfied – that we always want to be where we are not; she'd probably remind me too that faraway hills are green. Trouble was, I'd seen those hills – and I knew they were green.

Anyway, my mother was no longer there to tell me also that I was 'big and ugly enough' to sort things out for myself. She died at home in our old army house outside the barracks walls almost 25 years earlier, just a few months after my daughter, Sara, was born and given her name.

I went to my father's house on the north side of town. I opened all the doors and walked slowly through the empty rooms. Nothing remained to show that he had lived here. The walls had been stripped of their photographs and pictures; the mantelpiece held only a thin coating of dust; so too the sideboard.

My eye was caught by an unframed photograph thrown carelessly on top of a jumbled heap of old newspapers. It was my younger daughter, Georgia, her hands joined in smiling white-frocked innocence on the day, many years earlier, of her First Communion. I felt angry, seeing her so discarded; I pocketed the picture carefully, feeling as though I had rescued my daughter.

Upstairs, the wardrobes jangled with empty wire hangers when I swung open the doors. In the corner of one wardrobe was a forgotten pile of old college books and fading lecture notes. I stooped over the pile, thumbing my way slowly through the old books and dusty foolscap pages.

There among the books I found a small, white envelope with my own name on it, written in my own hand. I opened it with a kind of wonder.

Inside were a few scallop-edged black-and-white photos that must have been taken a few months after I left school, during my first term at college. About a dozen of us, boys and girls, smile out from the pictures; we have party hats on our heads – the occasion was a Christmas 'social' for a local club. Most of the faces I remember well, but a few are almost beyond recall. My own face looks so boyish that I might have been a schoolboy rather than a university student who was learning to drink and suffered from notions of how to run the world in a better way.

At least in the envelope and its contents I had found some fragment of myself in my father's house. In that empty house there was nothing else of me or for me. It had been a place to call at but I had never left it feeling enlarged, as though my life had been made greater by having been within it. Closing the front door behind me brought no sadness: the house was no more than a place where somebody I used to know had lived.

It is, I am sure, the simple desire *to belong* that binds fans to their own team. The team is greater than yourself but you too are made greater by your belonging. Colours and scarves and shirts tell the world of your membership of a larger, greater family.

If you're lucky, you also have your own kith and kin. In Dublin, on the way back, I visited my son in his office and, after day's end at the publishing company where he works, we went for a meal together. He had his own problems: he has, since he was a lad, followed the fortunes of Everton . . .Next day, Sara was at the airport to say goodbye to me. I could tell she was feeling lonely after she hugged me and turned away at the Departures entrance. I stood a while watching her through the plate-glass wall as she made her way along the footpath towards the bus stop for the coach back into the city. I rapped sharply on the glass with my fist and she looked up and I saw her face brighten into a smile as she spotted me. I hated to see her less than happy but you can't help feeling good too, that somebody cares about your leaving.

It made me think I was back in Wolverhampton before we had even left the ground: a complete Wolves tracksuit was making its way down the narrow aisle towards where I was sitting at the back of the plane. For a moment I thought it might be Robbie Keane or Dominick Foley returning to Molineux after a flying trip home but the young man in the familiar gold and black was unknown to me. He was in the company of two older men, around my own age; all three of them sat in the row directly across the aisle from my own seat.

I waited until we were airborne before leaning across the aisle to inquire if my neighbour and his companions were flying over for the game the following day.

I saw my fellow passenger's glance drop to my Wolves' tie and I saw the question in his own face.

It transpired that I was travelling along with Wolves' Irish scout. Willie Byrne lives in Dublin; somewhere in my diary his name and phone number were already written, given to me before I had first come to Wolverhampton by Pat Courtney, a former Shamrock Rovers player who had gone on to be sports editor of Independent Newspapers. I'd meant to ring; the Irish connection might lend an interesting line or two to my work. Somehow I'd never got round to phoning but now it didn't matter: that old Celestial Director had brought us together in the skies.

Like Pat Courtney, Willie had also played for Rovers. Now he was self-employed; the scouting was a labour of love which would be impossible were he employed in a regular nine-to-five job. He'd been reluctant to sever his talent-spotting links with Stoke City but a visit to Molineux had been enough to persuade him to throw in his lot with the Wanderers. On their behalf he clocked up thousands of miles checking out promising youngsters all over Ireland, north and south. Robbie Keane had given Wolves a higher profile in Ireland; Willie felt he could compete on level terms with Premiership scouts for the signatures of Ireland's best young footballers. The crucial factor in many parents' decision was the youth policy at Molineux: Irish mums and dads on exploratory visits to Wolverhampton nearly always felt that here their boys would not only be well trained for a footballing career but that they would also be safe, in the care of older hands and heads that knew life had to be lived off the pitch as well as on it.

More than the plane flew on that journey from Dublin to Birmingham. In the winking of an eye, it seemed, I was shaking hands and saying goodbye to Willie and his track-suited son and his travelling mate beside the baggage carousel at Birmingham International. All three of them were waiting on at the airport to meet a later flight from Cork: on board would be the mother and father of a young lad from the south of Ireland who had just signed on Molineux paper.

'I want them to get a taste of the Molineux atmosphere,' Willie said, grinning. 'It will be electric tomorrow.'

42

'There's Only One Keith Curle'

The match to which Willie Byrne was referring was the home game against Albion. Until I came to the Black Country, I had no idea of the intensity of this local rivalry. In terms of poisonous intentions and wrongs remembered, this local derby can be classed alongside the tribal civilities of Rangers and Celtic in Glasgow. If there is a saving grace to our Midlands hostilities, it is probably the absence of any pseudo-nationalist or distorted religiosity in the proceedings.

Molineux was packed for the game on that last Sunday in April. For Wolves, a good result was vital to our progress towards the play-offs. Before kick-off that day the contenders for the fifth and sixth play-off positions were placed as follows:

Place	Team	Games to Play	Points
5.	Bolton	2	72
6.	Wolves	4	70
7.	Watford	3	70

With two games in hand on Bolton, and one on Watford, we were in a position that our rivals must have envied. And yet, like every other fan, I knew only too well how fine the line was between success and failure. After the game against the Baggies, Wolves had to travel to Bolton and Grimsby before concluding the campaign with a home tie against

Bradford. It was a daunting run-in but, like most of the sell-out crowd that day, I was optimistic about the result. The Baggies were having a disastrous season, marooned in mid-table; there were rumours of trouble in their camp. It was time, we felt, for the wheel to turn; victory in the last three meetings between the sides had gone to Albion.

Elvis was on the loudspeakers, crooning 'The Wonder of You'. Molineux swung in the sunshine; thousands of voices did the ooh-ooh-ooh bit with gusto.

It struck me as an odd choice in music for the day: hardly the kind of song that the rival supporters would sing to each other.

It reminded me of Tom's story of the last, final, complete and utter ending to his marriage. Tom is a droll, dry-witted member of the Molineux press corps; he is also an undoubted Wolves lunatic — it's my guess that he emerged into the world from the womb fully clad in old-gold and black. His wife was less than enchanted with having to take second place to Wolves in her husband's affections.

With time running out for the marriage (as Tom himself recounts it) his disconsolate wife rounded on him in indignation.

'It's true,' she accused him, 'you love Wolves more than you love me.'

'Listen,' Tom told her, 'I love the fucking Albion more than I love you.'

After that it was red cards all round.

Molineux gave a verbal red card to the visitors: the announcement of every single name in the Albion line-up was ritually and roundly booed. There were other rituals to be enacted. A presentation to Mike Stowell to mark his record number of appearances in the Wolves goal. Wolfie's mock assault on the hapless Baggy Bird whom he up-ended on the Molineux turf . . .

And then the codology was over; hostilities commenced at one o'clock in the Molineux sunshine.

Colin had kept faith with the side that had won at St Andrew's: Muscat, Richards, Curle and Gilkes across the back; in midfield, Robinson, Sedgley, Emblen and Simpson; up front, Steve Corica playing a little behind Flo. Simon Osborn, back from suspension, was on the bench alongside Steve Bull; so too was Robbie Keane, making his first — and much welcomed — appearance after Nigeria.

Lee Hughes's kick-off was marked by a chorus of boos.

The Wolfpack, enchanted by Albion's miserable season, found even louder voice as they sang, 'The Shit are Going Nowhere!'

Albion took their revenge on the field. A Muscat–Hughes exchange of opinions on the edge of our box resulted in a free kick for Albion; Muzzy, perhaps distressed by this slur on his opinions, dissented so much that he was called out of the wall to be yellow-carded by the referee. The free kick was eventually taken and cleared but the ball was promptly returned and, following an uncharacteristic mix-up in a slack defence, Evans was allowed a free shot into Mike Stowell's net. First blood to the Baggies.

Oddly enough, you'd think it was Wolves that had scored: Molineux found its voice and got behind its heroes.

Just two minutes later it seemed we must be on level terms. Simmo, raiding on the left, put over a sweet centre and there at the far post, incredibly unmarked and in acres of space, was Steve Corica . . . I watched the Australian steady himself, I had my arms half-raised in triumph and then, beyond explanation, Steve's sliced kick spun across the face of the goal and out over the opposite sideline for a throw. Molineux's groan was loud and collective.

The afternoon seemed to darken. Ten minutes later, with only a half-hour gone, the Molineux lights were switched on.

Not long after that we were on level terms. Simpson was again involved, his free kick eventually reaching the far post where Carl Robinson was on hand, boot waiting, to dispatch the ball into the net. Molineux was on its feet: the result we longed for was now surely within our grasp.

Ten minutes into the second half, with the score unchanged, we were surer than ever. Muscat was fouled in the area by Kevin Kilbane and the ref., without hesitation, pointed to the spot. We were jubilant, counting our three points, gloating in our rightful victory over the Baggies.

Maybe Tom's ex-wife was sticking pins into a wax model of our Keith.

Molineux groaned again as Keith took a long run and skied the ball over the bar.

The Wolfpack was forgiving: they chanted 'There's only one Keith Curle', as though, by their generosity, they could lift Keith and his team to the victory we hungered for.

Robbie made his return after that, replacing Corica, but his jinking magic could not alter the scoreline. Even Bully's arrival, seven minutes from the end, in place of the injured Flo, could not swing the game our way. At the end it was the Albion fans who were singing, with heavy irony, 'There's only one Keith Curle!'

Poor Keith. A year before they had sung the same song when he had gifted the Baggies an own goal and victory.

Nobody in Molineux blamed him: it could have happened to a bishop . . .

★

The following night, again at Molineux, I watched Wolves Reserves squander a three-goal lead against their Barnsley counterparts in a game that ended 3–3. Wolves' third goal came from the penalty spot. As Mark Jones was lining up the kick, a few of the wags in the sparse attendance shouted down at the manager to show him how it was done. The Reserves' manager, of course, was Keith Curle. He turned round to the crowd, acknowledging the advice with a smile and a wave. He has chutzpah, does our Keith . . .

43

Return to the Reebok

The following night, on Tuesday, 27 April, Watford travelled to Port Vale. They won 2–1. It was their sixth successive win, lifting them into fifth place, a point ahead of Bolton and two points ahead of Wolves.

For the first time since 13 March, when we had beaten Bristol City 3–0, we were out of the top six. That win had lifted us into sixth place, just a single point ahead of Watford. Just over two weeks later, on the night we beat Crewe 3–0 at Molineux, we had stretched our lead over Watford to seven points. Now, in an astonishing turnaround, Graham

Taylor's men had won six games on the trot and leap-frogged above both ourselves and Bolton.

Listening to the Watford result on the radio that night, I felt a tiny stirring of panic inside me. The pale walls of the rented flat seemed suddenly cheerless; the emptiness of the flat was oppressive.

I needed the comfort of the company of my own kind: I had to share my unease with another Wolves lunatic.

I called Gerry.

'Don't worry,' he said. 'The Watford bubble has to burst. We'll be all right, just wait and see. Don't panic.'

How I wanted not to . . .

Two days later, on the Newbridge training ground, I could sense the change in the atmosphere. The sun was shining that morning but there was less *craic*, less banter than usual among the players.

I said as much to Colin.

'Yes,' he said, 'they're all very determined.'

He moved off then, taking over the supervision of the session from John Ward. Flo's knee was bandaged; my guess that we'd see Corica partner Robbie Keane up front for the game against Bolton would prove correct. The session, with its emphasis on defence, seemed to my amateurish eye, almost identical to the one I had watched on the freezing morning before the cup-tie against Bolton. Colin put the players through the moves with systematic carefulness: when the 'Bolton' attacker went through, Lee Naylor or whoever-it-was had to run into the designated spot while everybody watched. Not for the first time, I was intrigued: the whole thing was an exercise in imagination but here the imagined was made real, the possible spelt out. A whole series of moves and options were explored to counter the threat of a Bolton player called Cox. When the session was finished, I asked Colin about him.

'He's their right-back,' Colin told me. 'He pushes forward, like Emblen – and he also gets goals.'

His words hung in the bright sunshine like a threat.

Len was at the wheel for our trip to Bolton. To avoid Manchester's Friday evening traffic we ignored the exit arrows pointing off the M6 towards Bolton; instead we continued north along the motorway until we reached Junction 29, where we swung east on the M65. Within minutes we were heading south once more, this time on the M61. The white rigging of the Reebok hove into view on our left, like the topsails of some mysterious galleon, sailing through the Lancashire hills. It's a sight to take your breath away.

So was the scene inside the stadium. I was seated high up in the main stand, close to the spot from where I had watched the unforgettable drama of Wolves' 2–1 cup victory on 2 January. The action was a long, long way below me – but there is no 'bad seat' in the Reebok: everyone has a clear view of everything. The Wolfpack was in possession of the stand behind the goal on my right: they were heavily outnumbered by the home supporters but they made up in enthusiasm and commitment whatever they lacked in numbers.

Both qualities would be demanded of Wolves in this searching encounter; so would skill, nerve and ambition. The game was a classic 'six-pointer' – a win for either side would leave the loser trailing badly, probably out of the play-off race. Sky Television, anticipating the importance of the evening, had long since scheduled the clash for live transmission. Among the rapt audience glued to their TV sets throughout these islands was my own son – Adam would tell me the following day that a whole Dublin pub crowd, in recognition of their mate's father's lunacy, was lustily (and thirstily) rooting for Wolves throughout the match.

The game began in silence. It was an impressive silence. Alf Ramsey had died that day and for 60 seconds the entire stadium stood in soundless tribute to the man who had brought the World Cup to England. Our silence connected us with that vanished world of the '60s: for those silent seconds we switched on again in our minds the old black-and-white TV screens with their long-haired images of Best and Marsh and the Fab Four. Nothing stirred in the Reebok for that minute of remembrance; even the hills beyond the stadium seemed to bow their heads.

And then the ref. blew his whistle and the Reebok exploded and in the maelstrom of noise I knew we had a fight on our hands. Bolton were fighting for play-off survival. Back in mid-February, their 3–1 win over Albion – oh sweet statistic! – had left them in second place, a point ahead of Bradford and with a game in hand; automatic promotion had been within sight for Colin Todd's men. Bolton had held on to their second spot until 27 February: a 3–1 home defeat by lowly Crewe on that day had been the start of the Reebok rot. Four defeats in their next eight games had put automatic promotion beyond their grasp but they had steadied the ship, winning three of their four games before this Friday evening when, as the tabloids say, they were 'entertaining' our Molineux heroes.

The 'entertainment' was of the inhospitable kind. Wave upon white-shirted wave threatened to engulf Mike Stowell's goal in the opening minutes but somehow those waves were beaten back. I could sense, from my lofty perch, the jitters in the Wolves box; heedless fiddling about in those early minutes had me nervous and on the edge of my seat. I wanted to call our fellows together and remind them that they had prepared for this onslaught – hadn't I watched them work it all out on the training ground at Newbridge under Colin's managerial eye?

There was neither time nor space in the Reebok that Friday night for such reminders or consultations. But maybe our back eight remembered their homework anyway: they shipped plenty of punishment but they held the waves at bay. The home crowd grew frustrated; by the 20th minute the referee's wankership was being loudly and universally declared.

My own heart settled as local frustration intensified. On the half-hour Robbie raced through but he was forced wide on the end-line and his attempted curler was high and wide. Cue Bolton jeers of relief.

Nine minutes from half-time our defence forgot their Newbridge lessons and were surgically sliced apart by Bolton, leaving Gardner free to drive the ball high into the net past a falling Stowell's despairing hands.

The Reebok went wild: they had old scores to settle, not least our 2–1 victory over them in the Cup in early January. The wilder it got, the angrier I grew. I was seated on the extreme edge of the press area, next to the Bolton fans. On their feet, cheering and waving and shouting, they became odious to me. Truly, I wanted to ram their exultation down their throats. It gets you like that, this game of football. Even tight-lipped Alf had let his guard down all those years ago, when he had called the Argentines a bunch of animals . . .

It's the way the generals ensure that wars are fought. It's the basis of racism and religious bigotry: a refusal to look at the face of the man or woman you think is your enemy.

At half-time, with the score unchanged, I did just that: look my Bolton neighbour in the face. I'd been aware of him during the first half, on his feet or in his seat, cheering and punching the evening air, but I hadn't looked at him. Now, when I did, I saw a tall, distinguished-looking fellow in his mid-sixties with a thatch of silvery hair.

We talked. He was a local, he told me, but he'd been exiled to the isle of Anglesey for over 20 years; he'd fetched up on the island after a career at sea; now he was retired after working at the island's nuclear power station.

'It's a long haul from Holyhead to the Reebok,' I said.

My neighbour laughed. 'It's quicker to get to Dublin,' he said.

His words were a line of emotional latitude, strung across these islands, linking Dublin, Holyhead, Bolton and Wolverhampton. You cannot hate a man who smiles at you in the Lancashire evening and shows you pictures from his heartland. We went on talking while the seats emptied around us; our neighbours went in search of pies and hot drinks but I realised that my new-found friend was in search of richer nourishment. In the attentive ears of a stranger he had found a reason to trawl in his own past.

'I don't get to many away games anymore,' he told me. 'My son' — with a gesture he indicated the seat next to his own — 'sprang this trip on me as a birthday present.'

'You couldn't have a better one.'

'Maybe — probably not,' he said. 'The last time I saw Bolton take on Wolves was over forty years ago — Nat Lofthouse and Billy Wright were both playing that day.'

Sweet names from a sweeter past. William Ambrose looked forever westward from his pedestal outside Molineux but Nat Lofthouse was still alive and well, President of Bolton Wanderers.

Half-time ended, hostilities recommenced and my neighbour and I returned to our separate trenches. Yet it was not as before: it couldn't be, now that we had looked at each other's snapshots of past and present.

My neighbour even managed a rueful grin for me when Corica, capitalising on Phillips' hesitancy, put us on level terms after eight minutes of the second half.

Both sides made chances after that. Trandsen sent a Bolton free kick wide. Robbie had a shot deflected for a corner. Deeno conceded a corner that was cleared. Five minutes from the end, Mike Stowell made a stunning save from Taylor, diving to turn the ball around for a corner. Almost on the stroke of time Stowell saved us again, standing up to a rasper of such ferocity that it almost knocked him over.

It ended 1–1. My heart was still intact. So was our dream of making it into the play-offs. Bolton were still a point ahead of us but now they had only one game left whereas we still had two matches to play: win them and our place in the play-offs was assured. Colin Lee and John Ward knew it, pumping the Reebok air with clenched, excited fists. The Reebok knew it too – in their loud booing you could hear the sound of sourness.

My Anglesey Wanderer wasn't booing. He and I shook hands and he turned away with his son to take the road back to the island. At the top of the stand I lingered, savouring the moment. The evening air was honeyed; the lights on the hills behind the stadium were bright and welcoming, beacons on the road to the promised land.

The Wolfpack sensed it too. They were in no hurry to leave their dugout behind the goal. Like a triumphant army they were lined up, arms outstretched to taunt their fallen foes.

'BOLTON,' they chanted, 'YOU'RE GOING NOWHERE!'

We didn't know it then, but that old Celestial Director had other plans. We had foolishly offered our hostages to fortune and soon – very soon – we would pay the price of our presumptuousness.

44

The Lady of Shalott

That long, long season is recorded in half a dozen scrapbooks crammed with match reports, ticket stubs, team sheets and assorted bits and pieces of material connected to games up and down the country. The map of Grimsby that I picked up in the Information Centre is in the last of my scrapbooks; on the reverse of the page is a map of Cleethorpes. The gentle, pastel shades of the map convey no hint of the loud tackiness of the Cleethorpes seafront 'amusements' strip; neither does the map tell that it was here, finally, that we lost our way.

The match against Grimsby on Tuesday, 4 May, was our last away game of the season. When I decided to stay over at Grimsby that night

I was aware of my own wish to prolong, however briefly, this final journey. The roads of England had been incorporated into my personal atlas and I was reluctant to close the book on them.

I travelled alone, up the A449, heading east on the A5 before turning northwest on the A38, eventually joining the M1 at Junction 38. It was the route I followed on my weekly trips to Bretton Hall. I exited on to the M18, swinging east after a few miles on to the M180. I was in unexplored country, driving in the sunshine through Lincoln's green and pleasant land.

Life could not have been sweeter than it was on that sunny Tuesday afternoon. From Ireland the news was good – my son and my daughters had seemed busy and contented on our last round of phone calls. My head seemed finally to be getting rid of a stubborn cold that had lingered for almost two months. At Bretton Hall my work was progressing smoothly. I had paid Mrs Thatcher's Community Charge and had almost cleared my Visa balance. I had Mario Lanza to sing the miles away as I motored east towards Wolves' assignment with their destiny . . . Is it any wonder that I sang along with Mario in my Wolves-linked Corolla?

And I had the memory of the previous day at Newbridge to warm the cockles of my heart. In the morning sunshine the players responded to Colin's urgings with determination and good humour: the brittle tension of the previous week seemed to have been banished by the winning of our hard-earned point at Bolton. I'd waited until Colin had finished his Sky TV interview before venturing to join him as he left the pitch; our strolling progress was interrupted by a father and his boy, who wanted an autograph and a photo for the family album. I watched as Colin posed, smiling, with the boy and the father snapped and shook hands with Colin and wished him luck. It must be great, I said to Colin, to be able to make someone so happy so easily. His smile was answer enough as we resumed our leisurely progress towards the gate.

And then John Ward, in shorts and sweatshirt, came trotting up to join us. We chatted about Grimsby: the team were leaving that Monday afternoon and would stay overnight in a hotel close to the coast. Everyone I knew, I said, expected us to pick up three points – but Bradford, I asked, what about Bradford? I prefaced my words with an admission of my own lack of expertise but they were, I thought, the toughest team we had played, that December day up at the Valley Parade. 'Our team wasn't playing well then,' Colin said, and John murmured his agreement. 'It'll be different on Sunday. Don't forget that Bradford panicked on

Saturday' – Bradford had drawn 0–0 at home to Oxford – 'they took Mills off after an hour.'

I was in heaven that morning in Newbridge, the sun warming me, crossing the training pitches in the good-humoured company of these two men who were in charge of the team in old-gold and black. Not in my sweetest fantasies in Galway could I have painted such a scenario for myself.

I marvelled at the recollection of the encounter as I cruised towards Grimsby. The 'golden days' that Mario was singing about – the 'springtime of our happy youth' – were a long way behind me, but I had fresh golden days to warm me now: I had stumbled into an orchard where the fruit was sweet and the gardeners were generous.

I skirted the town of Grimsby, following the signs for Cleethorpes. 'Which Nationwide team plays all its matches away from home?' someone had asked me in Wolverhampton the week before and my blank expression had drawn the answer, 'Grimsby – their ground is in Cleethorpes.' Nearness to the ground was not my only reason for wanting to stay in Cleethorpes: there was also the sea. More than anything else about Galway, I missed the sea. Sometimes, skirting the ponds in West Park on an evening stroll, I would long for the sea: I had grown up within sight and sound of its ever-changing presence. On that journey to Grimsby the sea would be a gift to myself as the long season neared its end. I would go to sleep with its sound in my ears; in the morning I would walk beside it and taste its salt on my hungry lips, savouring the three points we expected to harvest.

If you threw a stone anywhere along the Cleethorpes promenade, you'd break the window of a B & B. I drove slowly up and down the seafront past a parade of Views and Lodges and Inns. I parked around the corner from the library and weighed up a couple of small hotels on a quiet street. I settled on the Mallow View, its name an echo of Ireland.

My choice would bring me face to face with more than an echo of myself.

'Why,' I asked the neat, diminutive, older woman as I was signing myself in, 'why is it called the Mallow View?'

'Because,' she said, 'it's where I come from.'

'Ah,' nodding my head. 'I'm from Galway myself.'

My landlady brightened.

'I know it well. My two nephews have hairdressing salons there.'

The rest was as easy as it was inevitable. I share my diminishing hairdressing custom between Conor and Reggie, two brothers with barber shops in Galway's main street. I have done so for some time; before that, in my youth, their father used to give me a trim.

The coincidence seemed like a happy omen: out here on the shoreline of the North Sea I had been greeted by a hand that carried with it the traces of my own, wilder shore. I took it, coming so soon after my unscripted encounter with Wolves' Irish scout, as yet another sign that the inscrutable CDF was smiling upon my odyssey. Invigorated by a brisk walk on the prom and a generous helping of Cleethorpes fish and chips, I was in good heart for our meeting with Grimsby that night.

★

At school in Galway we learned Tennyson's poem *The Lady of Shalott*. The lovely lady has been condemned to watching the world pass by on the road to Camelot only in the images reflected in her mirror; if she ever turns away from her glass to look, instead, at the reality, then the mirror will splinter and she will die. It might have been written for Molineux lunatics: we cherish our dream-images of the road to the Premiership but we keep our backs turned on the reality of results. I love the poem: sometimes, alone in the car, I find myself reciting remembered lines aloud :

> *On either side the river lie*
> *Long fields of barley and of rye . . .*

There is neither barley nor rye to be seen as you draw near to Blundell Park. Yet another McDonald's guards the approaches to the ground: a sign warns football fans not to park in the fast food joint's car-park. I found a place for the Corolla on the road to the left, alongside a terrace of neat, redbrick houses.

The night was cold. It would grow colder but we didn't know that then. As I made my way around the perimeter of the pitch to my allocated spot — I had gone to the wrong side of the ground, but they had let me in anyway and pointed me in the right direction — I was glad that I had decided to wear a warm coat: this wind from the North Sea left you in no doubt about where it came from.

I was early. The stands were empty save for a flock of stewards shepherded together at one end. There were lights in the windows of offices and what I took to be a stadium restaurant or bar. I stood aside near the corner flag to let a blazered guide pass by, leading his crocodile of corporate fans on a boy's night out. Blundell Park was stirring itself, getting ready for the action. It reminded me of Drama Society shows at college, long ago in Galway: half an hour before curtain up you'd peep out through the crack in the curtains and the tiny theatre in the grammar school would still be empty, rows of kitchen chairs unfilled, the two soft armchairs in the middle of the front row still waiting for the august bottoms of the president and his other half; yet not long after that you'd be doing your stuff on the tiny stage knowing that the darkness beyond the lights was filled with seated bums and clearing throats and applauding hands. At the end of those distant nights we took our bows to generous applause; here too, in Blundell Park, I hoped the night would close to the sound of cheers and clapping from the Wolfpack.

The locals, of course, had other ideas. The small, rusting stadium wasn't full but then it was a midweek game and besides, the Mariners were marooned in the middle of the table, safe from the currents of relegation but beyond the reach of the play-off lights. Their mediocrity seemed to spur their fans on. From the kick-off, Blundell Park cheered and jeered as if it were they and not us who were in contention for promotion.

I watched through a grid of peeling iron poles as Keane, lining out up front with Flo, forced a corner in the first minute. Nothing came of it, nor did anything come of the many other attacks we launched in that first half.

Part of the problem was a 19-year-old called Croudson in the Grimsby goal. The youngster, making his début in place of the absent Love, played like a man possessed. By talent. By courage. By his own dreams. Even by love . . .

And as one young man's dream blossomed, so I could feel ours beginning to wither in the frosty night. I could fault no one in our team for effort: they were trying, but their best seemed not to be good enough . . .

A couple of minutes from half-time we could have been sunk entirely in the North Sea. Jack Lester, attacking in our area, seemed to my partly obstructed view to be pulled back by Deeno; the Grimsby man managed to hold his balance, trying to shake Richards off; he succeeded in doing so but then, strangely, went down. The referee was deaf to Grimsby's loud and fervent demands for a penalty.

At half-time I spoke to a couple of stewards who had been on the touchline, close to the action. They were adamant that Grimsby had been denied a rightful penalty. 'He should've gone down when Richards was pulling him,' one said ruefully, shaking his head while the half-time crowd spilled around us in search of hot drinks and pies, 'he shouldn't have waited.'

The second half brought more of the same agony, the long, slow drift away from the play-offs. With a quarter of an hour to go, frozen in my seat at the top of the old wooden stand, I shut my eyes and tried to block out the frenzied noises of the scoreless drama unfolding around me: it was time for a private word with that old Celestial Director. Please, I prayed, please listen to me: give us this night the only goal we crave and lead us not away from the promised land of promotion . . . The CDF wasn't taking my calls that night.

Corica came on for Robbie with ten minutes to go: it was our last throw of the dice, a gamble that the little Australian would find again the magic touch that had given him goals at Birmingham and Bolton.

The travelling Wolfpack was baying for a score. And on the pitch Wolves surged forward, desperately seeking the winner. Three-and-a-half minutes from time Corica had a chance – but that night the magic was missing and his poor shot went wide. Seconds later Muscat found Emblen with a good centre but Neil's header was wide of the post. With a minute to go, Neil had another chance, but this time his header was over the bar.

The signal went up for time added on: three minutes. The locals booed: the prospect of a scoreless draw excited them.

In those three minutes nothing changed. And yet, when the referee finally brought the curtain down on the goalless drama, everything had changed. The Wolfpack was generous in its applause for the players and for Colin and John, but they were silent as they left the ground, filing out into the bitter night and the long road back to the Black Country. Like me, they knew that our path to the play-offs was no longer certain; events on other pitches would now determine whether we progressed beyond our final league game, at home to Bradford. I half wished I was travelling back again that night, back to the Midlands, where wounds could be licked in the privacy of home. Despite the lure of the sea, I had no wish to linger any longer on this refrigerated shore.

Wednesday, 5 May 1999: The Morning after Grimsby
The tide is in. The sea still stirs. The wind still blows. Even the sun is shining on this morning after the night before.

Life somehow still goes on. On this bright, breezy morning a great many people seem unaware that since last night a precious dream hangs by the flimsiest of threads. The proprietor of the Mallow View is chatty and cheerful when I check out, as though last night's affair at Blundell Park were no more than just another game. On the beach a middle-aged man cares only for his posse of ridiculous poodles. An elderly couple, he in anodyne anorak and she in scarlet windcheater over a floral frock, wish me good morning as though the world had not changed last night. The few other promenaders I meet pass by in silence, intent upon their personal universes, where draws at Blundell Park do not splinter into fragments the magic mirror in the dreamer's tower. A stout girl with a lovely face catches my eye as she jogs past, but in her fleeting smile I can find no trace of the tragedy of the night before.

I finish my comfortless walk and turn towards the shops.

The couple behind the counter in the newsagent's eye me warily as I leaf through one paper after another and I explain, apologetically, that I am searching for reports of the match. 'Ah, the game, you mean last night's?' And we are off then. We should have had a penalty, they say, and I agree with them, but then again, I remind them, you had young Croudson in goal. Ah yes, Croudson, he's only 19, you know. I know, I say, but still, I say, I could have murdered him last night. They laugh: they are my Cleethorpes kith and kin, they know the heart-scald of penalties refused and promotion disappearing like a shoreline. Wembley, the woman says dreamily, we were at Wembley — twice, her husband says, and their eyes sparkle with the memory of lover's labour won.

Their affability cannot lift me out of my valley of disappearing dreams. I turn the corner of the street but here there is no signpost to the land of heart's desire. On the promenade below me a bunker-like building is decorated with a pair of boards that read 'Lost Children' and 'Information' but even if I played the role of a lost child, the clerks inside the concrete bunker could not show us the way back to the twin towers of play-offs and promotion.

I am alone in Cleethorpes, but I know that I am not alone in my frustration. The Wolfpack everywhere is perplexed. The Viking pack and the German pack and all the rest of them wherever old-gold and black is prized will have heard the news by now, stunned at their internet keyboards, the grim news burned on their pitiless screens. A single game remains, but our salvation is no longer in our own hands: we must beat Bradford at Molineux and hope that Bolton stumble away to Portsmouth or that Watford come a cropper at home to Grimsby, our tormentors of last night. Like the Lady of Shalott we have been forced by destiny to turn and face the reality of an unforgiving world.

45

Truth in the Afternoon

I took the long way home to Wolverhampton that sunny Wednesday. I was in denial, even after my long walk on the Grimsby prom. Any distraction would serve, so long as it held at arm's length the cruel reality of the day. I had read the newspaper reports of the game; I had studied the revised league table. There was no need to: I could have compiled that table with my eyes closed as soon as the ref. had blown the final whistle the night before. For a few hours I wanted to forget the unforgettable. A longer road back would help; so would a race meeting.

Market Rasen was a name inscribed on the map of my childhood. It was a name that evoked memories of our kitchen in the Quarters in the barracks, the table hushed at tea-time as my shirt-sleeved father leaned close to the wireless while the static-laden voice of the BBC announcer droned his relentless way through racing results from another world: Pontefract, Chepstow, Doncaster . . . and Market Rasen. You could breathe and talk again when the results were done, when the day's winners and prices were finally marked in my father's neat script on the folded page of the *Irish Press*.

Now, Market Rasen was within hailing distance. The name had leaped out at me from the pages of the tourist brochure I had taken, with my map, from the Information Centre; minutes later, leafing through *The Guardian*, I had learned that racing would be held there that very day.

I experienced no epiphanies at Market Rasen; no door opened miraculously to disclose some startling insight into my army childhood. The racecourse is a bland, parkland affair; the meeting that day was polite and sparsely attended, a world away from the good-humoured hullabaloo of Ballybritt, the packed stands erupting as the leaders come up the hill for the last, lung-bursting furlong of the Galway Plate or the Galway Hurdle. Some things are the same, however: the bookies still finished up with my money in their satchels.

Still, the diversion served its purpose. When I pulled out of the car-park, the afternoon was almost done. For a few hours, at least, runners and riders, colours and prices had combined to keep my mind off the 'other' reality. After that I had to concentrate on roads that were new to me. The route I had chosen was circuitous; I went astray somewhere around Mansfield.

It was still bright when I turned off Tettenhall Road and swung in home. The flat was the same as I had left it. The photographs of my children still stared back at me from the mantelpiece. The books and folders were still piled neatly on the dining-table that doubled as my desk. My life was here, waiting for me to step back into it. Part of it anyway; I had merely taken another part on safari with me to Grimsby and Market Rasen and the rest of my journey. I let the silence of the flat settle upon me and I knew that reality wasn't so bad after all: I was home again, in the place where I wanted to be – and besides, you never knew, maybe the results would go our way on the last Saturday of the season . . .

On Saturday afternoon I picked Marcus up at the railway station in Wolverhampton. He'd flown in to Birmingham International the day before, from Galway, and had spent Friday night with friends in the city. Marcus is one of my best mates in Galway; it seemed entirely appropriate that, after all his threats and promises to come and watch my team in action, he should finally arrive in time for the last act of a long and gruelling drama.

Marcus and I grew up in the same sleepy backwater on the edge of

Galway. His home sat right on the shore of the bay, less than a half-mile from the barracks. We knew each other back then but he was too young and too little to be my pal: when you're twelve or thirteen years old, with the hormones kicking in, you tend not even to notice golden-haired sparrowfarts who are five years younger than you.

It was that shared background, however, which would eventually make us friends. That, and my own writing.

Marcus's mother and mine had been good friends back in the 1950s; I have more than one mental picture of her sitting beside my mother in our kitchen, drinking tea and talking – I suppose – about kids. Her span was brief: she was only in her thirties when she died. I think Marcus was about eight at the time of her death. Even as a child, I was aware of her going: my mother was sorrowful and, besides that, I missed the funny columns in the monthly religious magazine that she used to distribute.

When, years later, I came to write the story of my army boyhood, Marcus's mother became a central figure in one of the book's chapters. It had healing consequences that I could not have anticipated. For Marcus, those pages represented an astonishing glimpse of a mother he loved, but barely remembered. Life had cheated him of his mother; now, in a weird and wonderful way, some portion of her living presence had been given back to him in my book.

All this Marcus himself told me one wet afternoon in Galway a year or so after my book had been published. When we bumped into each other that day in the Eyre Square shopping centre, I had no idea that it would prove to be the start of a deep and solid friendship; we'd wave and sometimes chat briefly to each other in the street, but we didn't drink pints or coffee together and we certainly never exchanged confidences. That day in the shopping mall was different: Marcus wanted to talk to me about my book – and about his mother; I was grieving bitterly over a love affair that had gone wrong and I just wanted congenial company. We nattered for hours; we have been close mates ever since that fortunate day.

Marcus's presence in Wolverhampton for that last momentous game against Bradford held special resonances for me. My few mates back in Galway knew what I was doing in the Black Country but none had ventured into this territory that had become my own; none of them had walked these streets with me or looked with wonder at the Wanderers in action on the Molineux turf. Marcus's presence linked my other world with Wolverhampton; more than that, it marked the connection between my writing labours, between that other book and this one. I have hung my hat in many places and I have laboured in many vineyards but my work represents the seamless core at the heart of a life that has been fragmented and broken; Marcus's arrival at Wolverhampton station the day before the Bradford game was an affirmation of that thread of continuity.

Before we drove out to Marcus's B & B on Tettenhall Road, I had to show him our golden palace. I didn't try to conceal my proprietary pride as we circled the ground. I pointed out the shop as if it were a temple. I gestured towards Asda and told him the story of the jeans-clad executive guest who had gone shopping at George. I named the stands for him. We slowed to pay homage to William Ambrose . . .

That night we dined in a Bangladeshi restaurant in the shadow of St Peter's Church. Only one table was occupied when we arrived just after eight o'clock; the restaurant had filled and emptied by the time we rose from our table at one o'clock in the morning. The night was cool when we stepped out again on the street; even if it had been winter we would have felt no chill, warmed as we were by the embers of all the years we had raked across the dinner table. We were warmed with optimism, too, as we made our way towards home, that on the morrow all might yet be well.

I got my picture taken with Sir Jack about 20 minutes before the kick-off against Bradford. I'd written to his office months previously, explaining about my book assignment and requesting a brief meeting with the Master of Molineux. The circumstances of our brief encounter, however, ruled out any kind of meaningful exchange between us. I was ushered into his presence in a corridor on the top deck of the Billy Wright stand; through the half-open doors on either side of the corridor I caught a glimpse of rooms crowded with, I presumed, executive guests and special friends.

The club photographer materialised beside us. Rachel Heyhoe Flint asked if we were ready and the camera flashed while Sir Jack and I shook posed hands. For the brief moments we were together I could sense Sir Jack's nervousness. When I asked him what he thought of our prospects that day, he seemed to fidget with his words. 'We should have beaten the Baggies that day,' he said, and I could only presume that he was referring to Keith Curle's wayward penalty shot. He didn't seem too impressed by my assurance that we would win, Watford would stumble and all would yet be well. (In the press room they were similarly unimpressed by my unchanging predictions of Wolves victories.)

The ground was buzzing as we drew nearer to our final kick-off. That day you'd be hard put to it to squeeze an extra sardine into Molineux; even so, Lorraine Hennessy had come up trumps with a ticket for Marcus. He was somewhere behind me, I knew, up towards the top of the Billy Wright stand. The press box, too, was crammed. There was no Premiership football that Sunday, which meant that all the nationals had condescended to be represented. On one side of me was Terry Bosi, a former league referee who now looks after visiting referees and their assistants on Molineux match days. Ian Willars was on my left, with Tim Nash of the *Shropshire Star* two places further along. Between His Grace and Tim there was a stranger; this stranger and myself never exchanged a word, but it soon became irritatingly evident that he was a Bradford supporter let loose with a microphone.

Bradford kicked off amid an incredible, roof-raising din, infinitely louder than anything I had heard that season. All of Molineux knew what was at stake: on this last, 46th game of a long and gruelling season hung the outcome of the entire campaign. A victory would put us in the play-offs should Bolton or Watford fail to win; a draw would suffice if Bolton lost.

For Bradford the prize was even greater. Going into that last game they were in second place, a point ahead of Ipswich; a win would give them the second automatic promotion slot, regardless of what Ipswich did in their final game, at home to Sheffield. However, should Bradford lose or manage only to draw with Wolves, then an Ipswich win would deny Bradford automatic elevation.

The CDF, I figured, must have been in a particularly ironic, twisted mood when he wrote the script for the last day of the 1998–99 season.

Wolves made a panicky start, with both Curle and Gilkes frantically booting the ball into touch inside the first three minutes.

Bradford's travelling army, resplendent in their colours of amber and claret, did their best but they were outnumbered, out-roared and out-sung by the Wolfpack.

On the pitch, our men steadied themselves. In the Billy Wright stand I could hardly sit still.

In the 13th minute, Flo calmed our frayed nerves: as Emblen's header came back off the bar, our big Norwegian steadied himself to head home. One–nil to our side; Molineux was jubilant. Wembley lay just over the horizon.

Colin and John had decreed at their Friday press conference that the big screens at Molineux would carry no score-lines from elsewhere – 'We don't want the players distracted in any way' – but it didn't matter: thousands of radios were pressed to nervous ears on that critical afternoon. From somewhere behind me came the news that we didn't want to hear: Bolton were a goal up against Portsmouth. And then from over my other shoulder came more welcome news: Watford were losing 1–0 to Grimsby.

'Forget that stuff,' His Grace said. 'Just pay attention to what's going on here.'

I could have wept at what was going on. Twenty-five minutes had passed when Beagrie powered past Muscat and turned Keith Curle before shooting past Stowell. Overhead – I assure you this is true: I noted it at the time – the sky darkened with the threat of rain. The rain didn't fall but it might as well have done: five minutes before half-time Blake split the Wolves defence with a measured ball and Mills had an easy shot to put Bradford 2–1 ahead.

The interval was a glum quarter-hour. Even I, lunatic that I am, could feel a season slipping away from us; worse, it transpired that I should have heeded the Duke's advice about unconfirmed radio reports – Watford were, in fact, leading Grimsby 1–0.

Sometimes there's nothing you can do except sit there and take your punishment. Twenty minutes after the restart, Blake was given acres of room for a free shot in our area: Stowell had no chance. Bradford were within sight of the promised land; for us, there was nothing on view except another season in the Nationwide.

But the drama wasn't over. In the 77th minute Deeno brought Lawrence down in the box and Beagrie readied himself to shoot Bradford to a 4–1 lead.

Mike Stowell had other ideas, flinging himself to his right to tip the ball over for a superb save. We cheered him lustily, but it was consolation cheering by now – we knew it and Bradford's impatient army of supporters wanted desperately to believe it also.

Four minutes later Paul Simpson put the heart crossways in all of Bradford. Bully was given space in the box and the old schemer pushed the ball through to Simpson, who made no mistake with his left-foot shot.

Now Bradford were only a goal ahead and Wolves had seized the initiative.

Ipswich, the TV screen in the press room had told us at half-time, were leading Sheffield by three goals; all of Bradford, I was sure, knew it too. Another Wolves goal – and a draw – would see Ipswich vault above Bradford into the Premiership.

'Bradford,' I said to Ian, 'must be wetting themselves.'

The Wolfpack put it more colourfully.

'BRADFORD,' they chanted, 'YOU'RE SHITTING YOURSELVES!'

With six minutes to go, Blake and Beagrie were replaced for Bradford by Windass and Sharpe. A pair of geriatrics on zimmer frames would have managed to leave the pitch faster than the Bradford pair: anything would do now, anything which ticked away Bradford's 77-year absence from the top division of English football.

They almost didn't make it. With four minutes to go Simpson's rasper of a long-range free kick beat both defence and keeper but came back off the Bradford post. The gasps of relief could be heard in the furthest reaches of Yorkshire. (Ipswich didn't know at that precise moment how close they had come to the Premiership: the width of that Molineux upright sent them, and for the fourth year in a row, into the play-offs; for the fourth year in a row they went out at the semi-final stage, losing to Bolton Wanderers.)

The referee was still blowing the last post on our dreams when Paul Jewell and his managerial crew burst from the sideline to join the Bradford players in a love-fest of hugging and cheering and waving. On the lower deck of the opposite stand the Bradford fans were delirious, as if they could not grasp the enormity of their achievement. Forty-six games ago, nobody had given them a chance; now they had earned their passports to the Premiership.

In the centre circle of the pitch our own players sat slumped and dejected. For some of them it was the end of the road at Molineux; for Bully it might be the end of his footballing career – certainly he would never now grace the Premiership stage. Colin and John moved among them, back-slapping here, shaking hands there. They reminded me of undertakers at a funeral.

Some of them, I'm sure, must have wished the ground would open and swallow them, yet they roused themselves for one last hurrah, one last salutation to the followers who had never given up on them. The Wolfpack saluted them in return: this was a pain that was deeply felt but deeply shared also. We applauded as John and Colin shepherded their team from the pitch.

Bradford were in no hurry to leave: the singing and the cheering sounded as if they would go on forever. And I confess that at that time I hated them for their achievement. What right had they to flaunt their joy in front of us, on our pitch, in our town? The fist-punching exuberance of the Bradford fellow next to Ian was seriously getting on my wick.

'You're the senior man here,' I said to Ian. I knew I was being childishly spiteful, but I didn't care. 'Tell that guy to behave himself in the press box.'

His Grace was wiser than me, more generous, too, of spirit.

'They've been down for 77 years, Kevin,' he said to me. 'Let him have his celebration.'

I was rebuked, and properly so.

Out of the corner of my eye I caught sight of Marcus, five or six rows above me. We waved at each other, but I made no move to join him.

I sat alone for a long while as the stand emptied around me. I shut my eyes as if I could block out the finality of the day. Inside me I felt the cold numbness of loss. All season long I had never doubted that we would be promoted, as we'd climbed and fallen on the snakes-and-ladders of the league table. I had blindly kept the faith about the certainty of our success. It was as if I had believed that my very presence here was talismanic, assuring Wolves of their return to the glory of other days.

The truth was hard to swallow. I knew how hard those men in old-gold and black had fought for success; week after week in Newbridge frost and sunshine, I had watched them push themselves to their limits in the pursuit of fitness, skill and glory. I could have wept for them: they knew, as I knew, that their best had not been good enough. And yet I admired them; I would hear no word spoken against them. The old-gold and black were still – and always would be – colours to be worn with pride.

46

Journey's End?

I went back to Ironbridge a few weeks later. It was late afternoon; traffic was light. I found the car-park on the far side of the river and walked back over the historic iron bridge into the little town's main street. This time I needed no map to find the house: the directions I'd been given at the Information Centre last August, not long after my arrival in the Black Country, were still fresh in my mind. I followed the same roundabout route as I had on that first visit: left up the hill across the road from the tea shop, then cutting right through a high-walled narrow lane that ran vertically up the steep hillside between the backs of houses. At the top I paused for breath. It was easier then, downhill on the black-top road past elegant houses that dozed complacently in the evening sunlight.

The house I sought was on the left. It was red brick like its neighbours, small and compact. The blue plaque on the wall was the reason for my pilgrimage: it was here, on this Ironbridge hillside, that William Ambrose Wright had been born in 1924.

Back then, Billy Wright's house had been only half of the redbrick building: you could just make out where some later owners had bricked up another front door on the left to make a single dwelling out of the pair.

I didn't linger long. The street was deserted. You never knew when some of the discreet curtains might twitch and I might find myself having to explain to the local constabulary why an Irish scribbler was loitering on Belmont Road. Had I been asked, I would have been able to say only that it seemed the right place to be at the end of a Wandering season. In its quietness and in its modesty the little house reminded me of my own beginnings in the barracks. You carry those early years with you in your heart for the rest of your life, on all the roads of your life. My addiction to Wolves had its origins in those years spent in number two of the Married Quarters; now, at the end of the trail, I could see clearly that I had set out on this journey with the Wolves as a way of finding my way back to those old-gold early years. When I first set out on the journey, I had been only dimly aware of my innermost motives; now, at journey's end, on a Shropshire hillside, the workings of my own heart were clearer to me. You travel far to find again the golden place you set out from.

My father's lingering death and bugle-blown burial had shone a painful light into the darker corners of my own soul. I had mourned him, yes, but – as I have written earlier – I had lost him as a father many years before the bugler played the last post over his mortal remains. Yet there had been a time – a brief and golden span – when he had been my father: sometimes, in sweeter moments, he would help me with my reading, examine my spellings, check out my sums. To this day I can never look at the word 'rendezvous' without recalling that he taught me how to pronounce it when I first stumbled over its strangeness in a Kit Carson 64-pager.

It was in that time, too, that Wolves came cantering out of the sports pages of the *Sunday Press* to find a place in my heart. To follow those same Wolves, a lifetime later, was a way of tasting once more the nearly forgotten fruits of boyhood.

It was in those days, too, that William Ambrose had written his name on my boy's heart. Now, standing outside his childhood home, I was keeping my rendezvous both with him and with my own past.

Dreams will be dreamed as long as there are boys and girls to dream them; and in the same way, the Wolfpack will never abandon its hopes of achieving again the kind of greatness that had been won by the boy from this little house in Ironbridge.

When that day dawns, I want to be there to share in the joy, to exult in our return from exile. The ties that bind me to Galway are strong and vital – but they are not chains. I've no way of knowing if I could find a living in the Black Country, but I know that I intend to try. Granda Garvey of Lucan Street would understand, tipping me a wink from under the soft rim of his bushranger hat. The folk of this unsung country have made a place for me in their generous lives and it is in this place that I want to be.

The evening light was soft and peaceful over Shropshire as I set off down the hill to make my way towards Wolverhampton. Towards home.

Appendix 1

The Final Table 1998–99

| | P | HOME | | | | | AWAY | | | | | [Pts] |
		W	D	L	F	A	W	D	L	F	A	
Sunderland	46	19	3	1	50	10	12	9	2	41	18	105
Bradford	46	15	4	4	48	20	11	5	7	34	27	87
Ipswich	46	16	1	6	37	15	10	7	6	32	17	86
Birmingham	46	12	7	4	32	15	11	5	7	34	22	81
Watford	46	12	8	3	30	19	9	6	8	35	37	77
Bolton	46	13	6	4	44	25	7	10	6	34	34	76
Wolves	46	11	10	2	37	19	8	6	9	27	24	73
Sheffield Utd	46	12	6	5	42	29	6	7	10	29	37	67
Norwich	46	7	12	4	34	28	8	5	10	28	33	62
Huddersfield	46	11	9	3	38	23	4	7	12	24	48	61
Grimsby	46	11	6	6	25	18	6	4	13	15	34	61
WBA	46	12	4	7	43	33	4	7	12	26	43	59
Barnsley	46	7	9	7	35	30	7	8	8	24	26	59
Crystal Palace	46	11	10	2	43	26	3	6	14	15	45	58
Tranmere	46	8	7	8	37	30	4	13	6	26	31	56
Stockport	46	7	9	7	24	21	5	8	10	25	39	53
Swindon	46	7	8	8	40	44	6	3	14	19	37	50
Crewe	46	7	6	10	27	35	5	6	12	27	43	48
Portsmouth	46	10	5	8	34	26	1	9	13	23	47	47
QPR	46	9	7	7	34	22	3	4	16	18	39	47
Port Vale	46	10	3	10	22	28	3	5	15	23	47	47
Bury	46	9	7	7	24	27	1	10	12	11	33	47
Oxford Utd	46	7	8	8	31	30	3	6	14	17	41	44
Bristol City	46	7	8	8	35	36	2	7	14	22	44	42

Appendix 2

Appearances and Goals 1998–99

		League	FA Cup	Worthington Cup	Total
Atkins	apps	15	2	0(1)	17(1)
	gls	0	0	0	0
Bull	apps	11(4)	0	2	13(4)
	gls	3	0	3	6
Connolly	apps	18(14)	0(1)	2	20(15)
	gls	6	0	0	6
Corica	apps	20(11)	1	1(1)	22(12)
	gls	2	0	0	2
Curle	apps	45	1	3	49
	gls	4	0	0	4
Emblen	apps	30(3)	2	2(1)	34(4)
	gls	2	0	0	2
Ferguson	apps	2(2)	0	0(2)	2(4)
	gls	0	0	1	1
Flo	apps	18(1)	1	0	19(1)
	gls	5	1	0	6
Foley	apps	2(3)	0	0	2(3)
	gls	2	0	0	2
Froggatt	apps	8	0	2(1)	10(1)
	gls	0	0	0	0
Gilkes	apps	24(5)	2	0(1)	26(6)
	gls	0	0	0	0
Gomez	apps	18(2)	1	2	21(2)
	gls	2	0	0	2
Green	apps	1	0	0	1
	gls	0	0	0	0

		League	FA Cup	Worthington Cup	Total
Jones	apps	0(2)	0	0(2)	0(4)
	gls	0	0	0	0
Keane	apps	30(3)	2	4	36(3)
	gls	11	2	3	16
Muscat	apps	37	2	4	43
	gls	4	0	0	4
Naylor	apps	17(6)	0	4	21(6)
	gls	1	0	0	1
Niestroj	apps	2(3)	1	0	3(3)
	gls	0	0	0	0
Osborn	apps	36(1)	1	4	41(1)
	gls	2	0	1	3
Richards	apps	40(1)	1	4	45(1)
	gls	3	0	0	3
Robinson	apps	29(5)	2	1	32(5)
	gls	7	0	0	7
Sedgley	apps	41(3)	0(1)	3	44(4)
	gls	3	0	0	3
Simpson	apps	8(3)	0(1)	1	9(4)
	gls	2	0	0	2
Stowell	apps	46	2	4	52
	gls	0	0	0	0
Williams	apps	0	0	1	1
	gls	0	0	0	0
Whittingham	apps	9(1)	0	0	9(1)
	gls	1	0	0	1